Crochet Patterns

Crochet Patterns

Jean Kinmond

B. T. Batsford Limited
London
Charles T. Branford Company
Newton, Massachusetts 02159

© J. & P. Coats (U.K.) Limited 1969

First published 1969
Reprinted 1970
Reprinted 1971
7134 2636 5

U.S. edition 1969
Library of Congress Catalog Card Number 78–90356

Printed and bound in Great Britain by
William Clowes and Sons, Limited, London, Beccles and Colchester
for the publishers
B. T. Batsford Limited
4 Fitzhardinge Street, London W.1 and
Charles T. Branford Company
28 Union Street, Newton Centre, Massachusetts 02159

Contents

Introduction

'Fashion is a cycle', or 'nothing new under the sun'; how often these clichés have been repeated, yet today there is nothing more true. The fashions and even the songs of the twenties have been revived, but each given a new treatment and a 'with it' slant. In the twenties crochet was in fashion and found a place both in the wardrobe and the home. In the intervening years its application did not change with the times and it was considered old-fashioned and was even ridiculed by some as being only suitable for the antimacassars.

How tragic it was to lose these lovely traceries of lace, because there was no one capable of transforming crochet into contemporary trends.

Now the pendulum has swung and crochet is back with a tremendous impact. It all started in Italy, where the fashion designers realised that the stitches of crochet, both simple and elaborate, could be used with success to form the fabric of elegant blouses, dresses and suits.

The fashion grew in importance and spread to the salons of Paris and London. Interior decorators then saw how the lace patterns could be used to give the personal touch to the home and also add subtle decoration, by the use of mats, runners and other articles developed from the traditional stitches. This book contains a varied collection of designs both for the home and the wardrobe. So now it is possible for everyone to take part in the crochet renaissance. For the beginner clear and simple instructions and diagrams show all the stitches that will be needed.

JEAN KINMOND

Glasgow 1969

Instructions

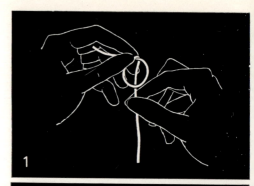

Hand positions

Right handed pupils work from right to left.

Left handed pupils work from left to right. The directions for each stitch apply to both right and left handed pupils.

For left handed pupils only; Place a pocket mirror to the left of each illustration and you will see the exact position in which you work reflected in the mirror.

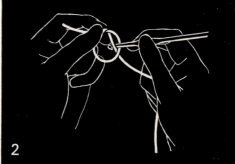

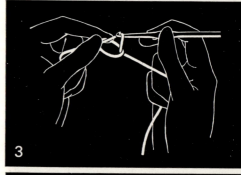

Step 1 - make a loop
1 Grasp thread near end between thumb and forefinger.
2 Make a loop by lapping long thread over short thread.
3 Hold loop in place between thumb and forefinger (Fig. 1).

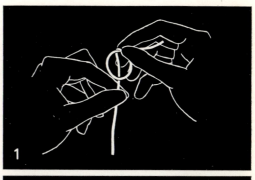

Step 2
1 Take hold of broad bar of hook as you would a pencil. Bring middle finger forward to rest near tip of hook.
2 Insert hook through loop and under long thread. Catch long end of thread (Fig. 2). Draw loop through.
3 Do not remove hook from thread.

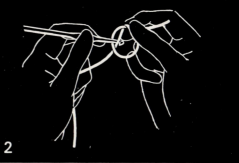

Step 3
1 Pull short end and ball thread in opposite directions to bring loop close around the end of the hook, but not too tight (Fig. 3).

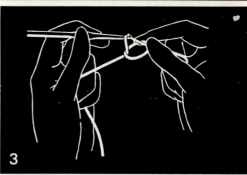

Step 4
1 Loop thread round little finger, across palm and behind forefinger (Fig. 4).

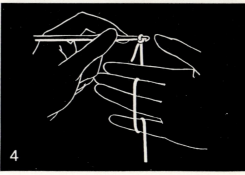

9

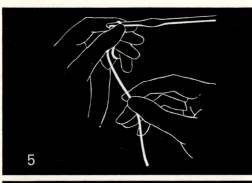

5

Step 5

1 Grasp hook and loop between thumb and forefinger.

2 Gently pull ball thread so that it lies around the fingers firmly but not tightly (Fig. 5).

3 Catch knot of loop between thumb and forefinger.

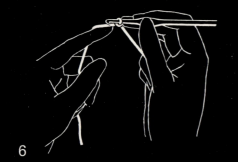

6

Step 6 CHAIN STITCH (Abbreviation – ch)

1 Adjust fingers as in Fig. 6 – the middle finger is bent to regulate the tension; the ring and little fingers control the thread. The motion of the hook in one hand and the thread in the other hand should be free and even. Ease comes with practice.

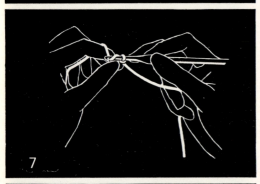

7

Step 7

1 Pass your hook under thread and catch thread with hook. This is called 'thread over' (Fig. 7).

2 Draw thread through loop on hook. This makes one chain (ch).

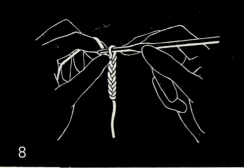

8

Step 8

1 Repeat Step 7 until you have as many chain stitches (ch sts) as you need – 1 loop always remains on the hook (Fig. 8).

2 Always keep thumb and forefinger near stitch on which you are working.

3 Practice making chain stitches until they are even in size.

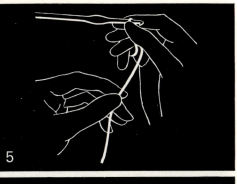

5

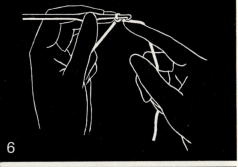

6

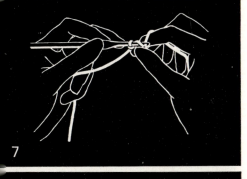

7

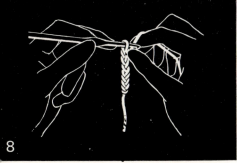

8

Slip stitch (abbreviation—ss)

Fig. 8a

Insert hook from the front under the 2 top threads of stitch to left of hook, catch thread with hook and draw through stitch and loop on hook (Fig. 8a).

Abbreviations

ch—chain; dc—double crochet; hlf tr—half treble; tr—treble; dbl tr—double treble; trip tr—triple treble; quad tr—quadruple treble; quin tr—quintuple treble; sp(s)—space(s); st(s)—stitch(es); ss—slip stitch; sp(s)—space(s)=2 ch, miss 2 ch or tr, 1 tr into next ch or tr; blk(s)—block(s)=4 tr plus 3 tr for each additional block in group.

★ Asterisk

Repeat instructions following the asterisk as many more times as specified in addition to the original. For example ★ 1 dc into next cluster, 1 dc into next loop, 2 ch, 1 tr into next dc, 2 ch, 1 dc into next loop; repeat from ★ 9 times more, means that there are 10 patterns in all.
Repeat instructions in parenthesis as many times as specified.
For example, '(3 ch, 1 dc into next sp) 5 times', means to make all that is in parenthesis 5 times in all.

Washing instructions

Coats Mercer-Crochet cotton

Use a warm lather of pure soap flakes and wash in the usual way, either by hand or washing machine. If desired, the article may be spin-dried until it is damp, or left until it is half dry. Place a piece of paper, either plain white or squared, on top of a clean, flat board. Following the correct measurements, draw the shape of the finished article on to the paper, using ruler and set square for squares and rectangles and a pair of compasses for circles. Using rustless pins, pin the crochet out to the pencilled shape, taking care not to strain the crochet. Pin out the general shape first, then finish by pinning each picot, loop or space into position.
Special points to note carefully when pinning out are:
(*a*) When pinning loops, make sure the pin is in the centre of each loop to form balanced lines.
(*b*) When pinning scallops, make all the scallops the same size and regularly curved.
(*c*) Pull out all picots.
(*d*) Where there are flowers, pull out each petal in position.
(*e*) When pinning filet crochet, make sure

that the spaces and blocks are square and that all edges are even and straight.
If the crochet requires to be slightly stiffened, use a solution of starch (1 dessertspoonful to 1 pint hot water), and dab lightly over the article. Raise the crochet up off the paper, to prevent it sticking as it dries. When dry, remove the pins and press the article lightly with a hot iron.

Orlon baby knitting

'Orlon' baby clothes wash very easily, either by hand or machine. Use your usual soap flakes or detergent. Rinse thoroughly and roll in a towel to remove excess moisture. Lay flat and leave to dry away from direct heat.

DO NOT IRON.

Tension

Check this carefully before commencing your design as only the correct tension will ensure the best finished specimens. If your crochet is loose use a size finer hook, if tight use a size larger hook.

Linens

Old Bleach coloured linens are available to match or tone with the following shades of Mercer-Crochet: White, 402 (Lt Rose Pink), 442 (Mid Buttercup), 459 (Mid Sky Blue), 477 (Tan), 503 (Coral Pink), 573 (Laurel Green), 575 (Mid Laurel Green), 594 (Steel Blue), 609 (Ecru), 610 (Dk Ecru), 621 (Lt French Blue), 623 (Spring Green), 625 (Lt Beige), 761 (Lt Forget-me-not), 535 (Navy Blue), Spec. 8918 (Lt Coral Pink).
Beau-Lin coloured linens are available to match or tone with the following shades of Mercer-Crochet: White, 441 (Buttercup), 442 (Mid Buttercup), 610 (Dk Ecru), 623 (Spring Green), 693 (Carnation Pink), 700 (Turkey Red), Spec. 8979 (Grey).

Coats Mercer-Crochet

A household word, Coats Mercer-Crochet possesses qualities which are of the utmost importance to the worker. It washes beautifully, never loses its colour or becomes 'stringy', is very elastic and preserves the beauty of the design. It is easy to work with, soft, glossy and of uniform thickness—it is the ideal crochet thread.

Crochet threads

Remember that texture plays an important

part in the beauty of crochet. The finer mercerised threads are more effective for the delicate designs used for table cloths, doilies, edgings and accessories, while the heavier threads are used for bedspreads, chairbacks, luncheon mats, etc.

Coats Mercer-Crochet is available in the following shades:

Ticket No. 3 White, 609 (Ecru), 610 (Dk Ecru).

Ticket No. 5 White, 609 (Ecru), 610 (Dk Ecru).

Ticket No. 10 White, Black, 608 (Tussah), 609 (Ecru), 610 (Dk Ecru), 442 (Mid Buttercup), 503 (Coral Pink), 621 (Lt French Blue), 623 (Spring Green), 625 (Lt Beige), Spec. 8918 (Lt Coral Pink).

Ticket No. 15 White, 609 (Ecru), 610 (Dk Ecru).

Ticket No. 20 White, 624 (Blush Pink), Spec. 8918 (Lt Coral Pink), 503 (Coral Pink), 2101 (Indian Pink), 693 (Carnation Pink), 402 (Lt Rose Pink), 439 (Rose Madder), 494 (Cerise), 854 (Petunia), 612 (Lt Amethyst), 690 (Pale Lavender), 459 (Mid Sky Blue), 508 (Lt Marine Blue), 594 (Steel Blue), 510 (Cobalt Blue), Spec. 8749 (Lt Navy Blue), 535 (Navy Blue), 680 (Pale Glacier Blue), 761 (Lt Forget-me-not), 621 (Lt French Blue), 521 (Jade), 942 (Apple Green), 623 (Spring Green), 573 (Laurel Green), 575 (Mid Laurel Green), 776 (Emerald Green), 463 (Parrot Green), 582 (Straw Yellow), 795 (Amber Gold), 962 (Dk Buttercup), 602 (Lt Cream), 608 (Tussah), 441 (Buttercup), 442 (Mid Buttercup), 513 (Orange), 538 (Marigold), 625 (Lt Beige), 609 (Ecru), 610 (Dk Ecru), 819 (Dk Beige), 2149 (Fawn Drab), 626 (String), 627 (Sand), 476 (Lt Brown), 477 (Tan), 579 (Brown), 836 (Nigger Brown), 417 (Lt Grey), Spec. 8979 (Grey), Black, 469 (Geranium), 700 (Turkey Red), 884 (Shaded Pink), 885 (Shaded Red), 889 (Shaded Lavender), 890 (Shaded Mauve), 891 (Shaded Lt Blue), 893 (Shaded Royal Blue), 892 (Shaded Dk Blue), Spec. 9532 (Shaded Jade), 894 (Shaded Emerald), 895 (Shaded Green), 901 (Shaded Lemon), 897 (Shaded Yellow).

Variegated—Spec. 8903, Spec. 8906, Spec. 8907, Spec. 8908, Spec. 9427, Spec. 9428.

Ticket No. 30 White, 609 (Ecru), 610 (Dk Ecru).

Ticket No. 40 403 (Rose Pink) and all shades except Spec. 8906, Spec. 9428.

Ticket No. 50 White, 609 (Ecru), 610 (Dk Ecru).

Ticket No. 60 All shades except 439, 463, 473, 510, 535, 579, 795, 819, 836, 854, 890, 892, 962, 2149, Spec. 8292, Spec. 8906, Spec. 8918, Spec. 9427, Spec. 9428, 447, 494, 626, 627, Spec. 8979.

Ticket No. 70 White, 609 (Ecru), 610 (Dk Ecru).

Ticket No. 80 White, 609 (Ecru), 610 (Dk Ecru).

Ticket No. 100 White, Black, 609 (Ecru), 610 (Dk Ecru).

Ticket No. 150 White, 610 (Dk Ecru).

Mounting crochet to linen

Launder crochet first as explained and pin to the required shape, ensuring that all lines of the crochet are accurate. Place crochet in correct position on linen and secure with pins. Run a line of basting stitches on the linen following the outline of the crochet edges which are to be attached to the linen. Remove Crochet.

Turn under a small hem, with fold lying on line of basting stitches and slipstitch. Overcast crochet to the hem.

Or

Cut fabric $\frac{1}{4}$ in. larger than required. Withdraw a thread $\frac{1}{4}$ in. from edge all round and turn back a small hem. Attach thread to any corner, 3 dc into same place, dc closely all round, working into space of drawn thread having 3 dc into each corner, 1 ss into first dc. The crochet edging may be sewn to edge of dc, or edging worked into dc, according to instructions.

Rows of double crochet (abbreviation —dc)

Note—In all crochet it is customary to pick up the 2 top loops (or threads) of each stitch as you work, unless otherwise specified.

Make a starting chain of 20 stitches for practice piece.

First row (1st row)

Fig. 9

Step 1 Insert hook from the front under the 2 top threads of 2nd ch from hook (Fig. 9).

Fig. 10

Step 2 Catch thread with hook—this is known as 'thread over' (Fig. 10).

Fig. 11

Step 3 Draw thread through chain. There are 2 loops on hook (Fig. 11).

Fig. 12

Step 4 Thread over (Fig. 12) and draw through 2 loops—1 loop remains on hook.

Fig. 13

Step 5 You have now completed 1 double crochet (dc) (Fig. 13).

Step 6 For next double crochet (dc) insert hook under 2 top threads of next ch and repeat Steps 2 to 6.

Step 7 Repeat Step 6 until you have made a double crochet (dc) in each ch.

Fig. 14

Step 8 At end of row of double crochet, work 1 ch (Fig. 14).
This 1 ch enables you to turn your work more easily but does not count as a stitch on next row.

Fig. 15

Step 9 Turn your work so that the reverse side is facing you (Fig. 15).

Second row (2nd row)

Step 1 Insert hook from the front under the 2 top loops of first stitch (st)—the last dc made on previous row.

Step 2 Catch thread with hook ('thread over') and draw through st—2 loops remain on hook.

Step 3 Thread over and draw through 2 loops—1 loop remains on hook.

Step 4 For next double crochet (dc), insert hook from the front under the 2 top loops of next st and repeat Steps 2 and 3.

Step 5 Repeat Step 4 until you have made a double crochet (dc) into each dc, 1 ch and turn.

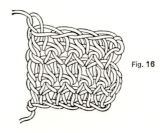

Fig. 16

Step 6 Repeat Second row (2nd row) until you are familiar with this stitch. Fasten off (Fig. 16).

How to 'fasten off'

Step 1 Do not make a turning chain at end of last row.

Step 2 Cut thread about 3 in. from work, bring loose end through the one remaining loop on hook and pull tightly (Fig. 16).

Rows of half treble crochet (abbreviation—hlf tr)

Notice when working rows of half treble (hlf tr) that there is an extra loop on the wrong side directly below the 2 top loops of each hlf tr. Work only into the 2 top loops of each stitch. Make a starting chain of 20 stitches for practice piece.

First row (1st row)

Fig. 17

Step 1 Pass hook under the thread of left hand (this is called 'thread over' Fig. 17).

Step 2 Insert hook from the front under the 2 top loops (or threads) of 3rd ch from hook.

Fig. 18

Step 3 Thread over hook and draw loop through ch (3 loops on hook), thread over (Fig. 18).

Fig. 19

Step 4 Draw through all loops on hook—1 loop remains on hook (Fig. 19). A half treble (hlf tr) is now completed.

Step 5 For next half treble (hlf tr), thread over, insert hook from front under the 2 top threads of next ch.

Step 6 Repeat Steps 3 to 5 until you have made a half treble (hlf tr) in each ch.

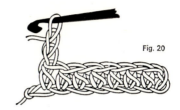

Fig. 20

Step 7 At end of row, 2 ch (Fig. 20) and turn.

The turning 2 ch does not count as a stitch on the following rows.

Second row (2nd row)

Step 1 Thread over hook, insert hook from front under the 2 top loops of first stitch (st)—the last hlf tr on previous row.

Step 2 Thread over hook and draw through stitch—there are 3 loops on hook, thread over and draw through all loops on hook.

Step 3 For next half treble (hlf tr), thread over hook, insert hook from the front under the 2 top loops of next stitch (st) and repeat Step 2.

Step 4 Repeat Step 3 until you have made a half treble (hlf tr) in each hlf tr, 2 ch and turn.

Step 5 Repeat Second row (2nd row) until you are familiar with this stitch. Fasten off at end of last row (Fig. 16).

Rows of treble crochet (abbreviation —tr)

Make a starting chain of 20 stitches for practice piece.

First row (1st row)

Fig. 21

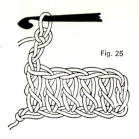

Fig. 25

Step 1 Thread over, insert hook from the front under the 2 top threads of 4th ch from hook (Fig. 21).

Fig. 22

Step 2 Thread over and draw through stitch (st). There are now 3 loops on hook (Fig. 22).

Fig. 23

Step 3 Thread over and draw through 2 loops—2 loops remain on hook (Fig. 23).

Fig. 24

Step 4 Thread over again and draw through the 2 remaining loops—1 loop remains on hook. One treble crochet (tr) is now completed (Fig. 24).

Step 5 For next treble crochet (tr), thread over, insert hook from the front under the 2 top loops of next stitch (st) and repeat Steps 2 to 5 until you have made a treble crochet (tr) in each st.

Step 6 At end of row, 3 ch (Fig. 25) and turn. The 3 turning ch stand as 1 tr and count as the first st in the following row.

Second row (2nd row)

Step 1 Thread over, insert hook from the front under the 2 top loops of the 5th stitch from the hook (2nd stitch on previous row).

Step 2 Repeat steps 2 to 7 of first row. Repeat the second row until you are familiar with this stitch. Fasten off.

How to 'turn your work'

In rows of crochet a certain number of chain stitches are added at the end of each row to bring the work into position for the next row. Then the work is turned so that the reverse side is facing the worker. The number of turning chain depends upon the stitch with which you intend to begin the next row.

Turning chain

dc — 1 ch
hlf tr — 2 ch
tr — 3 ch
dbl tr — 4 ch
trip tr — 5 ch
quad tr — 6 ch
quin tr — 7 ch

The above list gives the number of turning ch for each type of stitch which would be used when the following row is to be commenced with the same stitch. When applied to any of the stitches bracketed, the turning ch also stands as the first stitch of the next row.

16

Rounds of double crochet

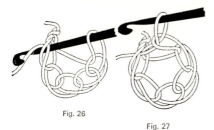

Fig. 26

Fig. 27

Step 1 Make a chain (ch) of 6 stitches (sts). Join with a slip stitch (ss) into 1st ch to form a ring (Figs 26 and 27).

Fig. 28

Step 2—1st row Make 8 double crochet (dc) into ring (Fig. 28). Place a safety pin in the last dc of 1st row to mark end of row. Move the safety pin to the last dc of the following rows.

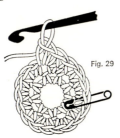

Fig. 29

Step 3—2nd row 2 double crochet (dc) into each dc of previous row—an increase made in each dc. There are 16 dc on row (Fig. 29).

Step 4—3rd row ★ 2 double crochet (dc) into next dc—an increase made in last dc (Fig. 29), 1 dc into next dc; repeat from ★ all round (24 dc on row).

Continue working in rows of double crochet as required, working increases wherever necessary in order to keep work flat and ending last row with 1 ss into each of next 2 dc. Fasten off.

Double treble (abbreviation—dbl tr)

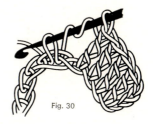

Fig. 30

Pass hook under the thread of left hand twice, insert hook into stitch to left of hook, thread over hook and draw through stitch (4 loops on hook) (Fig. 30). Thread over hook and draw through 2 loops on hook, thread over hook and draw through other two loops on hook, thread over and draw through remaining 2 loops (1 loop remains on hook).

Triple treble (abbreviation—trip tr)

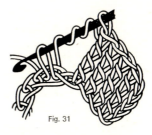

Fig. 31

Pass hook under the thread of left hand 3 times, insert hook into stitch to left of hook, thread over hook and draw through stitch (5 loops on hook) (Fig. 31). Thread over hook and draw through 2 loops on hook, (thread over hook and draw through other 2 loops on hook) 3 times, 1 loop remains on hook.

Quadruple treble (abbreviation—quad tr)

Pass hook under the thread of left hand 4 times and complete in same manner as trip tr until only 1 loop remains.

Quintuple treble (abbreviation—quin tr)

Pass hook under the thread of left hand 5 times and complete in same manner a strip tr until only 1 loop remains.

17

Picot (abbreviation—p)

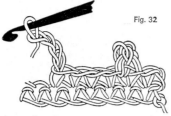

Fig. 32

Make a ch of 3, 4 or 5 sts according to length of picot (p) desired, join ch to form a ring working 1 dc into foundation or first ch (Fig. 32).

Clusters (abbreviation—cl)

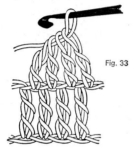

Fig. 33

Clusters may be worked in the following ways:

(a) A cluster worked over a given number of sts. Leaving the last loop of each on hook, work 1 dbl tr into each of next 4 sts, thread over hook and draw through all loops on hook (a 4 dbl tr cluster made) (Fig. 33).

Fig. 34

(b) A cluster worked into one stitch. Leaving the last loop of each stitch on hook, work 3 or more stitches into same stitch on previous row, thread over and draw through all loops on hook (Fig. 34).

(c) A cluster worked into loop or space. Leaving the last loop of each stitch on hook, work 3 or more stitches into space or loop on previous row, thread over and draw through all loops on hook (Fig. 35).

Fig. 35

Filet crochet

The following four stitches are used mostly in Filet Crochet and are referred to as spaces, blocks, lacets and bars.

Space (abbreviation—sp)

Fig. 36

Spaces are made with 2 ch, miss 2 stitches, 1 tr into next stitch (Fig. 36).

Blocks and spaces (abbreviations—blks and sps)

Fig. 37

Work 1 tr into each of next 4 stitches, 2 ch, miss 2 stitches, 1 tr into next stitch, 1 tr into each of next 3 stitches (Fig. 37).

Bar and lacet

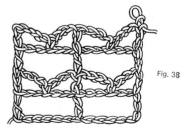

Fig. 38

(a) A bar consists of 5 ch, miss 5 stitches or a lacet, 1 tr into next stitch.

(b) A lacet consists of 3 ch, miss 2 stitches, 1 dc into next stitch, 3 ch, miss 2 stitches, 1 tr into next stitch (Fig. 38).

Puff stitch

Commence with desired length of ch, having a multiple of 3 ch plus 2.

1st row Draw loop on hook up $\frac{3}{8}$ in., thread over hook, insert hook into 8th ch from hook and draw loop up $\frac{3}{8}$ in., (thread over hook, insert hook into same st and draw loop up as before) 5 times, thread over and draw through all loops on hook, 1 ch to fasten (a puff stitch made), ★ 2 ch, miss 2 ch, thread over hook, insert hook into next ch and draw thread up $\frac{3}{8}$ in., (thread over hook, insert hook into same place and draw thread through as before) 5 times, thread over and draw through all loops on hook, 1 ch to fasten (another puff stitch made); repeat from ★ omitting a puff stitch at end of last repeat, 1 tr into last ch, 3 ch turn.

2nd row ★ Puff stitch into next sp, 2 ch; repeat from ★ omitting 2 ch at end of last repeat, 1 tr into 5th of 7 ch, 5 ch, turn.

3rd row ★ Puff stitch into next sp, 2 ch; repeat from ★ ending with 1 tr into 3rd of 3 ch, 3 ch, turn.

4th row ★ Puff stitch into next sp, 2 ch; repeat from ★ ending with 1 tr into 3rd of 5 ch, 5 ch, turn.
Repeat 3rd and 4th rows for length required, omitting turning ch at end of last row.

Tricot

Using a Tricot hook, commence with desired length of chain.

1st row Insert hook into 2nd ch from hook and draw thread through, ★ insert hook into next ch and draw thread through; repeat from ★ to end.

2nd row Thread over hook and draw through one loop on hook, ★ thread over and draw through two loops on hook; repeat from ★ to end.

3rd row Insert hook into horizontal stitch at back of 2nd upright stitch on previous row and draw thread through, ★ insert hook into horizontal stitch at back of next upright stitch and draw thread through; repeat from ★ to end.
Repeat 2nd and 3rd rows for length required, ending with 2nd row.

Crochet hooks

These are the correct numbers of steel hooks to use with Coats Mercer-Crochet:

Mercer-Crochet	Milward Steel Crochet Hook
No. 3 No. 5	1·75 (No. 2)
No. 10 No. 15	1·50 (No. 2½)
No. 20 No. 30	1·25 (No. 3)
No. 40 No. 50	1·00 (No. 4)
No. 60 No. 70	0·75 (No. 5)
No. 80 Nos 100 and 150	0·60 (No. 6)

These are the correct numbers of 'Disc' hooks to use with Coats Synthetic yarns:

Yarns	Milward Disc Crochet Hooks
Carefree Bri-Nylon 3 ply	3·50 (No. 9)
Carefree Bri-Nylon 4 ply	4·00 (No. 8)
Cadenza Courtelle 4 ply	3·50 (No. 9)
Caravelle Acrilan Double Crepe	4·00 (No. 8)
Spinelle Orlon Double Knitting	4·50 (No. 7)
Cadenza Courtelle Double Knitting	4·50 (No. 7)
Carefree Bri-Nylon Double Knitting	5·00 (No. 6)
Carefree Bri-Nylon Baby Quick Knit	5·00 (No. 6)
Coats Baby Orlon	3·50 (No. 9)

Coats Synthetic Knitting Yarns are equally suitable for crochet. In order to obtain the best tension with each of the yarns it is essential to use the correct type and size of crochet hook and reference to the table provided should be made before commencing.

Crochet hook size comparison chart

As from 1 July 1969, European Crochet hook manufacturers will be changing over to the New International Standard Range of crochet hooks. This chart shows both present and new ranges. The new range is illustrated in actual size, with the new size numbers alongside. There will be a changeover period of three to four years, at the end of which the old sizes will be withdrawn. Where the New International Standard Range has at present equivalents in steel and Disc (aluminium) crochet hooks, the steel hooks will be phased out. From this chart it will be easy to make comparisons between the old sizes as well as the new sizes which will be referred to in patterns in future.

Important—Crochet workers should observe one basic rule: this is to adhere to the 'tension' stated in the instructions as only the correct tension will ensure the best result. It is desirable to work with the size of crochet hook quoted as this has been selected as the most suitable size for the thickness of yarn being used. If your tension is loose use a size finer hook, if tight use a size larger hook.

By reference to the comparison chart it will be seen that the new range provides an adequate number of sizes to work all old patterns and to obtain the 'tension' required.

Milward new range of steel and aluminium crochet hooks. These hooks are shown in actual size with Present as well as New International numbering.	New Range International	Present Range Steel	Present Range Disc (aluminium)
		8	
		7	
		6½	
0.60 Milward 6	0.6	6	
		5½	
0.75 Milward 5	0.75	5	
		4½	
1.00 Milward 4	1	4	
		3½	
1.25 Milward 3	1.25	3	
1.50 Milward 2½	1.5	2½	
1.75 Milward 2	1.75	2	
		1½	
2.00 Milward 14	2	1	14
		1/0	13
2.50 Milward 12	2.5	2/0	12
3.00 Milward 11	3	3/0	11
			10
3.50 Milward 9	3.5		9
4.00 Milward 8	4		8
4.50 Milward 7	4.5		7
5.00 Milward 6	5		6
5.50 Milward 5	5.5		5
6.00 Milward 4	6		4
7.00 Milward 2	7		2

Tablecloth

First motif

Commence with 6 ch, join with a ss to form a ring.

1st row 3 ch, 11 tr into ring, 1 ss into 3rd of 3 ch.

2nd row 1 dc into same place as last ss, * 3 ch, 1 dc into next tr; repeat from * 10 times more, 1 ch, 1 hlf tr into first dc.

3rd row * 4 ch, 1 dc into next loop; repeat from * ending with 4 ch, 1 ss into hlf tr of previous row. (12 loops.)

4th row 1 ss into first loop, 4 ch, leaving the last loop of each on hook work 2 dbl tr into same loop, thread over and draw through all loops on hook (a 2 dbl tr cluster made), * 5 ch, a 3 dbl tr cluster into next loop; repeat from * ending with 5 ch, 1 ss into top of first cluster.

5th row 1 ss into each of next 2 ch, 4 ch, a 2 dbl tr cluster into sp, * 7 ch, a 3 dbl tr cluster into next sp; repeat from * ending with 7 ch, 1 ss into top of first cluster.

6th row 1 dc into same place as last ss, * 5 ch, into next sp work a 3 dbl tr cluster 5 ch and a 3 dbl tr cluster, 5 ch, 1 dc into top of next cluster; repeat from * omitting 1 dc at end of last repeat, 1 ss into first dc.

7th row 1 ss into each of next 2 ch, 1 dc into loop, * 3 ch, into next 5 ch sp work 6 dbl tr with 1 ch between each, 3 ch, 1 dc into each of next 2 loops; repeat from * omitting 1 dc at end of last repeat, 1 ss into first dc.

8th row * 3 dc into next sp, (1 dc into next dbl tr, 3 ch, 1 dc into top of last dc—picot made) 5 times, 1 dc into next dbl tr, 3 dc into next sp; repeat from * ending with 1 ss into first dc. Fasten off.

Second motif

Work same as first motif for 7 rows.

8th row * 3 dc into next sp, (1 dc into next dbl tr, picot) twice, 1 dc into next dbl tr, 1 ch, 1 ss into centre picot of corresponding point on first motif, 1 ch, 1 dc into top of last dc on second motif, (1 dc into next dbl tr, picot) twice, 1 dc into next dbl tr, 3 dc into next sp; repeat from * once more, and complete as for first motif.

Make 10 rows of 10 motifs joining adjacent sides as second was joined to first, leaving one point free on each motif between joinings.

Filling

1st row Attach thread to centre picot of free point between motifs, 6 ch, 4 dbl tr with 2 ch between each into same picot, * 4 ch, miss 3 picots, leaving the last loop of each on hook work 1 trip tr into next picot, 1 trip tr into first free picot after joining of motifs, thread over and draw through all loops on hook (a joint trip tr made), 4 ch, 5 dbl tr with 2 ch between each into centre picot of next point; repeat from * twice more, 4 ch, a joint trip tr over picots on each side of joining of motifs, 4 ch, 1 ss into 4th of 6 ch.

2nd row 1 dc into same place as last ss, (2 dc into next sp, 1 dc into next dbl tr) twice, 8 ch, 1 dc into 3rd ch from hook, 1 dc into each of next 5 ch, 1 ss into dc on top of dbl tr, * (2 dc into next sp, 1 dc into next dbl tr) twice, 4 dc into next sp, 1 dc into joint trip tr, 4 dc into next sp, 1 dc into next dbl tr, (2 dc into next sp, 1 dc into next dbl tr) twice, 7 ch, remove hook, insert hook into turning ch of bar and draw loop through, 1 ch, miss 1 ch, 1 dc into each of next 6 ch, 1 ss into dc on top of dbl tr; repeat from * twice more, (2 dc into next sp, 1 dc into next dbl tr) twice, 4 dc into next sp, 1 dc into joint trip tr, 4 dc into next sp, 1 ss into first dc. Fasten off.

Fill in all spaces between motifs in same manner.

Damp and pin out to measurement.

Coats  Mercer-Crochet No. 40 (20 grm).
10 balls. This model is worked in shade 625
(Lt Beige), but any other shade of Mercer-
Crochet may be used.
Milward steel crochet hook 1·00 (No. 4).

Size of motif 3½ in. in diameter
Measurement 35 in. square

Tablecloth

Edging

Commence with 23 ch.

1st row 1 dbl tr into 11th ch from hook, 3 ch, miss 3 ch, 1 dbl tr into each of next 9 ch, 4 ch, turn.

2nd row Miss first dbl tr, 1 dbl tr into each of next 8 dbl tr, 3 ch, 1 dbl tr into next dbl tr, 3 ch, miss 3 ch, 1 dbl tr into next ch, 4 ch, turn.

3rd row (3 dbl tr into next sp, 1 dbl tr into next dbl tr) twice, 3 ch, miss 3 dbl tr, 1 dbl tr into next dbl tr, 3 ch, miss 3 dbl tr, 1 dbl tr into top of turning ch, 7 ch, turn.

4th row Miss first dbl tr and 3 ch, 1 dbl tr into next dbl tr, 3 ch, 1 dbl tr into each of next 8 dbl tr, 1 dbl tr into top of turning ch, 7 ch, turn.

5th row Miss first 4 dbl tr, 1 dbl tr into next dbl tr, 3 ch, miss 3 dbl tr, (1 dbl tr into next dbl tr, 3 dbl tr into next sp) twice, 1 dbl tr into 4th of turning ch, 4 ch, turn.

Repeat 2nd to 5th row until there is sufficient to go along one side of cloth, ending with 2nd row then work 3rd, 4th, 5th and 2nd rows once more. Fasten off. Join thread into 4th of turning ch of last row worked, 7 ch, 1 dbl tr into top of next dbl tr of next row-end, 3 ch, 1 dbl tr into base of same dbl tr, 3 dbl tr over row-end, 1 dbl tr into top of next dbl tr, 3 dbl tr over next row-end, 1 dbl tr into top of turning ch of next row-end, 4 ch, turn.

Continue from 2nd row and work other 3 sides to correspond. Fasten off. Oversew foundation ch to side of last 4 rows.

Outer edging

Attach thread to first st of dbl tr group to left of any corner, 1 dc into same place, ★ 1 hlf tr into next st, 1 tr into next st, 1 dbl tr into next st, 1 trip tr into next st, 4 ch, 1 ss into top of last trip tr (picot made), 1 dbl tr into next st, 1 tr into next st, 1 hlf tr into next st, 1 dc into next st, into next sp work 1 dc 1 hlf tr 1 tr and 1 dbl tr, 1 trip tr into next st, 4 ch, 1 ss into top of last trip tr, into next sp work 1 dbl tr 1 tr 1 hlf tr and 1 dc, over next row-end work 1 dc 1 hlf tr 1 tr and 1 dbl tr, 1 trip tr into next st, 4 ch, 1 ss into top of last trip tr, over next row-end work 1 dbl tr 1 tr 1 hlf tr and 1 dc, continue in this manner to corner, into next sp work 1 dc 1 hlf tr 1 tr and 1 dbl tr, 1 trip tr into next st, 4 ch, 1 ss into top of last trip tr, into corner sp work 1 dbl tr 1 tr 1 hlf tr 2 dc 1 hlf tr 1 tr and 1 dbl tr, 1 trip tr into next st, 4 ch, 1 ss into top of last trip tr, into next sp work 1 dbl tr 1 tr 1 hlf tr and 1 dc, 1 dc into next st; repeat from ★ all round ending with 1 ss into first dc. Fasten off.

Slipstitch to edge of gingham.
Damp and press.

2 balls Coats  Mercer-Crochet No. 40 (20 grm). 1 yd 36 in. wide gingham. Milward steel crochet hook 1·00 (No. 4).

Tension 4 sps and 4 rows = 1 in.

Measurement 36 in. square approx.

Lay a small hem all round edge of gingham and sew in position.

Coffee table mat

Commence with 5 ch.

1st row 1 tr into 5th ch from hook, ★ 1 ch, 1 tr into same place as last tr; repeat from ★ 7 times more, 1 ch, 1 ss into 3rd of 5 ch (10 sp).

2nd row 4 ch, 1 tr into first sp, ★ 1 ch, 1 tr into next tr, 1 ch, 1 tr into next sp; repeat from ★ ending with 1 ch, 1 ss into 3rd of 4 ch.

3rd row 5 ch, ★ 1 tr into next tr, 2 ch; repeat from ★ ending with 1 ss into 3rd of 5 ch.

4th row As 2nd row.

5th and 6th rows As 3rd row.

7th row 3 ch, 1 tr into same place as last ss, ★ 4 ch, leaving the last loop of each on hook work 2 dbl tr into top of last tr, thread over and draw through all loops on hook (a 2 dbl tr cluster made), 5 ch, a 2 dbl tr cluster into 5th ch from hook, miss 1 tr, 2 tr into next tr; repeat from ★ omitting 2 tr at end of last repeat, 1 ss into 3rd of 3 ch. Fasten off.

8th row Attach thread to sp between first 2 clusters, 1 dc into same place as join, ★ (5 ch, a 2 dbl tr cluster into 5th ch from hook) twice, 1 dc into sp between next 2 clusters; repeat from ★ omitting 1 dc at end of last repeat, 1 ss into first dc. Fasten off.

9th row Attach thread to sp between first 2 clusters, 3 ch, 1 tr into same place as join, ★ 7 ch, 2 tr into sp between next 2 clusters; repeat from ★ ending with 7 ch, 1 ss into 3rd of 3 ch.

10th row 1 ss into next tr, 1 ss into next ch, 4 ch, ★ (miss 1 ch, 1 tr into next ch, 1 ch) 3 times, miss 2 tr, 1 tr into next ch, 1 ch; repeat from ★ omitting 1 tr and 1 ch at end of last repeat, 1 ss into 3rd of 4 ch.

11th row 5 ch, ★ 1 tr into next tr, 2 ch; repeat from ★ ending with 1 ss into 3rd of 5 ch.

12th and 13th rows As 7th and 8th rows.

14th row As 8th row.

15th to 17th row As 9th to 11th row.

18th row As 7th row.

19th to 21st row As 8th row.

22nd to 24th row As 9th to 11th row.

25th row 1 dc into first sp, ★ 7 ch, miss next sp, 1 dc into next sp, (3 ch, miss next sp, 1 dc into next sp) 3 times; repeat from ★ omitting 1 dc at end of last repeat, 1 ss into first dc.

26th row 1 ss into 7 ch loop, 3 ch, 8 tr into same loop, ★ 1 dc into next 3 ch sp, (3 ch, 1 dc into next 3 ch sp) twice, 9 tr into next 7 ch loop; repeat from ★ ending with 1 dc into next 3 ch sp, (3 ch, 1 dc into next sp) twice, 1 ss into 3rd of 3 ch.

27th row 6 ch, 1 dc into 4th ch from hook, ★ (1 tr into next tr, 3 ch, 1 dc into top of last tr) 7 times, 1 tr into next tr, 2 ch, 1 dc into next 3 ch sp, 4 ch, 1 dc into 4th ch from hook, 1 dc into next 3 ch sp, 2 ch, 1 tr into next tr, 3 ch, 1 dc into top of last tr; repeat from ★ omitting 1 tr 3 ch and 1 dc at end of last repeat, 1 ss into 3rd of 6 ch. Fasten off.

Damp and pin out to measurements.

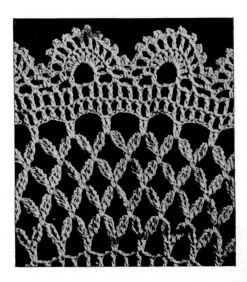

Pottery by Primavera, London, S.W.3

Coats 🞉 Mercer-Crochet No. 10 (20 grm). 4 balls. This model is worked in shade 621 (Lt French Blue), but any other shade of Mercer-Crochet may be used.
Milward steel crochet hook 1·50 (No. 2½).

Tension 4 rows tr 2 in. in diameter.

Measurement 19 in. in diameter.

29

Coffee table mat

Daisy motif

Inner circle (first motif)

With Buttercup, commence with 2 ch.
1st row 8 dc into 2nd ch from hook, 1 ss into first dc. Fasten off.

2nd row Attach White to first dc, ★ 8 ch, 1 dc into 2nd ch from hook, 1 hlf tr into next ch, 1 tr into each of next 5 ch, 1 ss into next dc; repeat from ★ working last ss into same place as thread was attached. Fasten off.

Second motif

Work first row same as first motif.

2nd row Attach White to first dc, 8 ch, remove hook, insert hook into tip of petal on first motif and draw dropped loop through, 1 dc into 7th of 8 ch, 1 hlf tr into next ch, 1 tr into each of next 5 ch, 1 ss into next dc, 8 ch, remove hook, insert hook into tip of next petal on first motif and draw dropped loop through, 1 dc into 7th of 8 ch, 1 hlf tr into next ch, 1 tr into each of next 5 ch, 1 ss into next dc and complete as for first motif.
Make and join 25 more motifs in same manner, joining 2 petals of one motif to 2 petals of adjacent motif leaving 2 petals free on each side of joining, and joining last motif to first motif as before. Attach White to tip of petal at left of any joining, 1 dc into same place, ★ 5 ch, 1 dc into tip of next petal on same motif, 3 ch, 1 dbl tr into joining of 2 motifs, 3 ch, 1 dc into tip of next petal; repeat from ★ all round omitting 1 dc at end of last repeat, 1 ss into first dc. Fasten off.
Attach White to tip of petal at left of any joining on other side of motifs, 1 dc into same place, ★ 7 ch, 1 dc into tip of next petal on same motif, 5 ch, 1 dbl tr into joining of 2 motifs, 5 ch, 1 dc into tip of next petal; repeat from ★ all round omitting 1 dc at end of last repeat, 1 ss into first dc. Fasten off.

Outer circle

Make and join 45 motifs. Attach White to tip of petal at left of any joining, 1 dc into same place, ★ 5 ch, 1 dc into tip of next petal on same motif, 5 ch, 1 dbl tr into joining of 2 motifs, 5 ch, 1 dc into tip of next petal; repeat from ★ all round omitting 1 dc at end of last repeat, 1 ss into first dc. Fasten off.

Damp and press.

To make up

Cut a piece of linen 19½ in. in diameter. Make a narrow hem all round. Pin inner circle centrally on to linen. Cut away surplus material at back of motifs leaving ⅛ in. for hem on each side. Turn back hems to wrong side and sew hems and inner circle neatly in place. Sew outer circle in place.

Damp and press.

Coats  Mercer-Crochet No. 20 (20 grm).
2 balls White and 1 ball 962 (Buttercup). This model is worked in these two shades, but any other shades of Mercer-Crochet may be used.
Piece of Old Bleach linen, C 55 (Sky), 21 in. square.
Milward steel crochet hook 1·25 (No. 3).

Size of motif 1⅜ in.
Measurement 21½ in. approx. in diameter.

Luncheon mats

Coats ✿ Mercer-Crochet No. 10 (20 grm).
7 balls Dark Ecru 610.
or Clark's ⚓ Anchor Pearl Cotton No. 8 (10 grm).
18 balls Ecru 0388/610. (Use double thread).
This model is worked in above shade, but any other shade of Mercer-Crochet or Pearl Cotton may be used.
Milward steel crochet hook 1·50 (No. 2½).
The above quantities are sufficient for 2 place mats.
Size of motif Mercer-Crochet 3½ in. square.
Pearl Cotton 3¾ in. square.
Measurements Mercer-Crochet 15 in.× 11½ in.
Pearl Cotton 16 in.× 12¼ in.

Place mat (make 2)

First motif

Commence with 12 ch, join with a ss to form a ring.

1st row Into ring work 24 dc.

2nd row Picking up back loop of each dc work 1 dc into each dc.

3rd row 1 dc into first dc, ★ 11 ch, miss 5 dc, 1 dc into next dc; repeat from ★ twice more, 11 ch, 1 ss into first dc.

4th row Into first loop work 15 dc, 1 ch, turn (petal started).

5th row Picking up back loop of each dc work 1 dc into each dc, 1 ch, turn.

6th row Picking up back loop of each dc work 1 ss into first dc, 1 dc into each of next 13 dc, 1 ss into next dc, 1 ch, turn.

7th row As 5th row.

Repeat 6th and 7th rows 4 times more having 2 dc less after each repeat.

Fasten off. Attach thread to next loop on 3rd row and work second petal in same manner. Work two more petals over next 2 loops in same manner. Do not fasten off at end of last petal, turn.

16th row 1 dc into first dc, ★ 9 ch, miss 3 dc, 1 dc into next dc of same petal, 11 ch, miss 7 row-ends of petal, 1 dc into next row-end, 1 dc into 4th row-end of next petal, 11 ch, 1 dc into first dc of last row of petal; repeat from ★ omitting 1 dc at end of last repeat, 1 ss into first dc.

17th row ★ 11 dc into next loop, 15 dc into each of next 2 loops; repeat from ★ 3 times more.

18th row Picking up front loop of each dc, ★ work 1 dc into each of next 11 dc, miss 1 dc, 1 dc into each of next 13 dc, miss next 2 dc, 1 dc into each of next 13 dc, miss 1 dc; repeat from ★ 3 times more.

19th row Picking up back loop of each dc ★ work (1 dc into each of next 3 dc, 3 ch, 1 dc into same place as last dc) 3 times, 1 dc into each of next 2 dc, miss 1 dc, 1 dc into each of next 6 dc, 3 ch, 1 dc into same place as last dc, 1 dc into each of next 5 dc, miss 2 dc, 1 dc into each of next 6 dc, 3 ch, 1 dc into same place as last dc, 1 dc into each of next 5 dc, miss 1 dc; repeat from ★ 3 times more, 1 ss into first dc. Fasten off.

Second motif

Work same as first motif for 18 rows.

19th row Picking up back loop of each dc work (1 dc into each of next 3 dc, 3 ch, 1 dc into same place as last dc) twice, 1 dc into each of next 3 dc, 1 ch, 1 ss into corresponding loop on first motif, 1 ch, 1 dc into same dc on second motif, 1 dc into each of next 2 dc, miss 1 dc, 1 dc into each of next 6 dc, 1 ch, 1 ss into corresponding loop on first motif, 1 ch, 1 dc

into same dc on second motif, 1 dc into each of next 5 dc, miss 2 dc, 1 dc into each of next 6 dc, 1 ch, 1 ss into next loop on first motif, 1 ch, 1 dc into same dc on second motif, 1 dc into each of next 5 dc, miss 1 dc, 1 dc into each of next 3 dc, 1 ch, 1 ss into next loop on first motif, 1 ch, 1 dc into same dc on second motif and complete same as first motif.

Make 3 rows of 4 motifs, joining adjacent sides as second motif was joined to first motif.

Edging

1st row Working along one long side, attach thread to corner 3 ch loop of end motif, 1 dc into same place as join, ★ 4 ch, 1 dc into next 3 ch loop, ★ (8 ch, 1 dc into next 3 ch loop) 3 times, 8 ch, miss next 2 loops, 1 dc into next 3 ch loop; repeat from last ★ twice more, (8 ch, 1 dc into next 3 ch loop) 3 times, (4 ch, 1 dc into next 3 ch loop) twice, ★ (8 ch, 1 dc into next 3 ch loop) 3 times, 8 ch, miss next 2 loops, 1 dc into next 3 ch loop; repeat from last ★ once more, (8 ch, 1 dc into next 3 ch loop) 3 times, 4 ch, 1 dc into next loop; repeat from first ★ once more, omitting 1 dc at end of last repeat, 1 ss into first dc.

2nd row 3 ch, 1 tr into same place as last ss, ★ 1 tr into each ch to corner, 2 tr into corner dc; repeat from ★ omitting 2 tr at end of last repeat, 1 ss into 3rd of 3 ch.

3rd row 1 dc into same place as last ss, ★ 3 ch, miss 1 tr, 1 dc into next tr, 3 ch, miss 2 tr, 1 dc into next tr, ★ 4 ch, miss 3 tr, 1 dc into next tr; repeat from last ★ 29 times more, 3 ch, miss 2 tr, 1 dc into next tr, (3 ch, miss 1 tr, 1 dc into next tr) twice, 3 ch, miss 2 tr, 1 dc into next tr, ★ 4 ch, miss 3 tr, 1 dc into next tr; repeat from last ★ 21 times more, 3 ch, miss 2 tr, 1 dc into next tr, 3 ch, miss 1 tr, 1 dc into next tr; repeat from first ★ once more, omitting 1 dc at end of last repeat, 1 ss into first dc.

4th row Into each loop work 2 dc 3 ch and 2 dc, 1 ss into first dc. Fasten off.

Damp and pin out to measurements.

Coats ⚙ Mercer-Crochet No. 20
(20 grm).
4 balls. This model is worked in shade
610 (Dark Ecru), but any other shade
of Mercer-Crochet may be used.
Milward steel crochet hook 1·25
(No. 3).
The above quantity is sufficient for 1
centrepiece, 2 place mats and 2 glass mats.

Tension Centre motif $1\frac{1}{2}$ in. in diameter.
Measurements
Centrepiece $16\frac{1}{2}$ in. in diameter.
Place mat 10 in. in diameter.
Glass mat $5\frac{1}{2}$ in. in diameter.

Luncheon mats

Luncheon mats

Centrepiece

Centre motif

Commence with 10 ch, join with a ss to form a ring.

1st row 1 dc into ring, ★ 4 ch, leaving the last loop of each on hook work 3 dbl tr into ring, thread over and draw through all loops on hook (a cluster made), 4 ch, 1 dc into ring; repeat from ★ 4 times more, 4 ch, a 4 dbl tr cluster into ring. (6 petals made.)

2nd row ★ 8 ch, 1 ss into 5th ch from hook, 5 ch, 1 ss into same ch as last ss, 4 ch, 1 ss into same place as last ss, 3 ch, 1 ss into top of next cluster; repeat from ★ ending with last ss into top of first cluster. Fasten off.

3rd row Attach thread to first 5 ch loop, 1 dc into same place as join, ★ 14 ch, 1 dc into next 5 ch loop; repeat from ★ ending with 14 ch, 1 ss into first dc.

4th row 18 dc into each 14 ch loop, 1 ss into first dc.

5th row ★ 1 dc into next dc, 3 ch, miss 2 dc; repeat from ★ ending with 1 ch, 1 tr into first dc. (36 loops.)

6th row ★ 4 ch, 1 dc into next loop; repeat from ★ ending with 1 ch, 1 tr into tr of previous row.

7th and 8th rows As 6th row.

9th row ★ 5 ch, 1 dc into next loop; repeat from ★ ending with 2 ch, 1 tr into tr of previous row.

10th to 12th row As 9th row ending last row with 5 ch, 1 ss into tr of previous row.

13th row Into each loop work 7 dc, 1 ss into first dc. Fasten off.

14th row *First motif.* Work same as centre motif for one row, 8 ch, 1 ss into 5th ch from hook, 2 ch, 1 dc into 4th of 7 dc on 13th row, 2 ch, 1 ss into same place as last ss, 4 ch, 1 ss into same place as last ss, 3 ch, 1 ss into top of next cluster on motif, 8 ch, 1 ss into 5th ch from hook, 2 ch, 1 dc into 4th of next 7 dc on 13th row, 2 ch, 1 ss into same place as last ss, 4 ch, 1 ss into same place as last ss, 3 ch, 1 ss into top of next cluster on motif and complete as for 2nd row. Fasten off.

Second motif

Work same as centre motif for one row, 8 ch, 1 ss into 5th ch from hook, 2 ch, 1 dc into first free 5 ch loop after joining of previous motif, 2 ch, 1 ss into same place as last ss, 4 ch, 1 ss into same place as last ss, 3 ch, 1 ss into top of next cluster, 8 ch, 1 ss into 5th ch from hook, 2 ch, miss next 7 dc loop, 1 dc into 4th of next 7 dc, 2 ch, 1 ss into same place as last ss, 4 ch, 1 ss into same place as last ss, 3 ch, 1 ss into top of next cluster, 8 ch, 1 ss into 5th ch from hook, 2 ch, 1 dc into 4th of next 7 dc, 2 ch, 1 ss into same place as last ss, 4 ch, 1 ss into same place as last ss, 3 ch, 1 ss into top of next cluster and complete as for first motif. Fasten off.

Make 10 more motifs in same manner joining each as second was joined to first

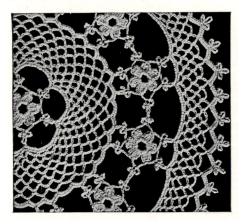

and to 2 loops of 13th row as before leaving one loop of 7 dc free between each motif (*see illustration*).

15th row Attach thread to first free 5 ch loop on one motif, 1 dc into same place as join, ★ 8 ch, 1 dc into next 5 ch loop on same motif, 16 ch, 1 dc into first free 5 ch loop on next motif; repeat from ★ omitting 1 dc at end of last repeat, 1 ss into first dc.

16th row ★ 12 dc into next 8 ch loop, 24 dc into next 16 ch loop; repeat from ★ ending with 1 ss into first dc.

17th row 1 dc into same place as last ss, ★ 3 ch, miss 3 dc, 1 dc into next dc; repeat from ★ ending with 1 ch, 1 tr into first dc. (108 loops.)

18th to 25th row As 6th to 13th row.

26th row As 14th row having 27 motifs instead of 12 and missing 2 loops instead of one between motifs.

27th row Attach thread to first free 5 ch loop on one motif, 1 dc into same place as join, ★ 8 ch, 1 dc into next 5 ch loop on same motif, 12 ch, 1 dc into first free 5 ch loop on next motif; repeat from ★ omitting 1 dc at end of last repeat, 1 ss into first dc.

28th row ★ 12 dc into next 8 ch loop, 20 dc into next 12 ch loop; repeat from ★ ending with 1 ss into first dc.

29th row 1 dc into same place as last ss, ★ 3 ch, miss 3 dc, 1 dc into next dc; repeat from ★ ending with 1 ch, 1 tr into first dc. (216 loops.)

30th to 32nd row As 6th to 8th row.

33rd row ★ 7 ch, miss one loop, 1 dc into next loop; repeat from ★ ending with 7 ch, 1 ss into tr of previous row.

34th row Into each loop work (7 dc, 5 ch, 1 ss into top of last dc, 6 ch, 1 ss into

same dc, 5 ch, 1 ss into same dc, 6 dc), 1 ss into first dc. Fasten off.

Place mat (make 2)

Work same as centrepiece for 20 rows.

21st and 22nd rows As 33rd and 34th rows of centrepiece.

Glass mat (make 2)

Work same as centrepiece for 12 rows, ending 12th row with 2 ch, 1 tr into tr of previous row.

13th and 14th rows As 33rd and 34th rows of centrepiece.

Damp and pin out to measurements.

Trolley cloth

First motif

Using Lt Rose Pink, commence with 7 ch, join with a ss to form a ring.

1st row Into ring work 12 dc, 1 ss into first dc.

2nd row 3 ch, 1 tr into same place as last ss, 2 tr into each dc, 1 ss into 3rd of 3 ch. Break off and join Lt Beige.

3rd row 4 ch, leaving the last loop of each on hook work 2 dbl tr into same place as last ss, thread over and draw through all loops on hook (a cluster made), ★ 7 ch, miss 2 tr, a 3 dbl tr cluster into next tr; repeat from ★ 6 times more, 7 ch, 1 ss into first cluster.

4th row 6 ch, 1 tr into same place as last ss, ★ 1 tr into each of next 7 ch, 1 tr 3 ch and 1 tr into top of next cluster; repeat from ★ omitting 1 tr 3 ch and 1 tr at end of last repeat, 1 ss into 3rd of 6 ch.

5th row 1 ss into first sp, 4 ch, into same sp work a 2 dbl tr cluster 5 ch and a 3 dbl tr cluster, ★ 5 ch, 1 dc into centre tr of tr group, 5 ch, into next sp work a 3 dbl tr cluster 5 ch and a 3 dbl tr cluster; repeat from ★ omitting a cluster 5 ch and a cluster at end of last repeat, 1 ss into top of first cluster. Break off and join Lt Rose Pink.

6th row 1 ss into first sp, 4 ch, into same sp work a 2 dbl tr cluster (3 ch, a 3 dbl tr cluster) twice, ★ 4 ch, leaving the last loop of each on hook work 1 dbl tr into each of next 2 loops, thread over and draw through all loops on hook, 4 ch, into next sp work (a 3 dbl tr cluster, 3 ch) twice and a 3 dbl tr cluster; repeat from ★ omitting (a cluster, 3 ch) twice and a cluster at end of last repeat, 1 ss into top of first cluster.

7th row 1 dc into same place as last ss, ★ (5 ch, 1 dc into top of last dc—picot made—3 dc into next sp, 1 dc into

top of next cluster) twice, 5 ch, 1 dc into top of last dc, 4 dc into each of next 2 loops, 1 dc into top of next cluster; repeat from ★ omitting 1 dc at end of last repeat, 1 ss into first dc. Fasten off.

Second motif

Work as for first motif for 6 rows.

7th row 1 dc into same place as last ss, 5 ch, 1 dc into top of last dc, ★ (3 dc into next sp, 1 dc into top of next cluster, 2 ch, 1 ss into corresponding picot on first motif, 2 ch, 1 dc into top of last dc) twice, ★ 4 dc into each of next 2 loops, (1 dc into top of next cluster, 2 ch, 1 ss into corresponding picot on first motif, 2 ch, 1 dc into top of last dc, 3 dc into next sp) twice and complete as for first motif. Make 4 rows of 6 motifs, joining adjacent sides as second motif was joined to first motif, leaving 2 free picots between motif joinings.

Filling

Work as for first motif for 2 rows, do not break off thread.

3rd row 4 ch, 1 dbl tr into same place as last ss, 2 ch, 1 ss into any free picot between 4 motifs, 2 ch, 1 dc into top of last dbl tr, 4 ch, 1 ss into same place as last dbl tr, ★ 1 ss into each of next 3 tr, 4 ch, 1 dbl tr into same place as last ss, 2 ch, 1 ss into next free picot, 2 ch, 1 dc into top of last dbl tr, 4 ch, 1 ss into same place as last dbl tr; repeat from ★ 6 times more, 1 ss into each of next 3 sts. Fasten off.
Fill in all sps between motifs in this manner.

Damp and press.

Coats ❁ Mercer-Crochet No. 40
(20 grm).
2 balls 402 (Lt Rose Pink) and 1 ball
625 (Lt Beige). This model is worked
in these two shades, but any other
shades of Mercer-Crochet may be
used.
Milward steel crochet hook 1·00
(No. 4).

Size of motif $3\frac{1}{4}$ in. in diameter.
Measurements 13 in. × $19\frac{1}{2}$ in.

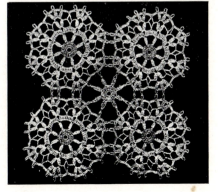

Tray cloth

Diagonal cross

First section

Commence with 21 ch.

1st row 1 dc into 5th ch from hook, 1 dc into each of next 7 ch, 3 dc into next ch, 1 dc into each of next 8 ch, 4 ch, turn.

2nd row (Lifting back half of each st), miss first dc, 1 dc into each of next 8 dc, 3 dc into next dc, 1 dc into each of next 8 dc, 4 ch, turn.

Repeat last row 21 times more. (23 rows.) Fasten off.

Second section

Work as first section for 22 rows. Now join as follows:

23rd row (Lifting back half of each st), miss first dc, ★ insert hook into next dc and into corresponding dc on previous section and complete as for a dc; repeat from ★ 8 times more, complete row on second section only. Fasten off.

Third section

Work as for previous section.

Fourth section

Work as for previous section joining adjacent sides to form diagonal cross.

Small ring

1st row Wind Mercer-Crochet 4 times round end of a pencil, remove from pencil and work 24 dc into ring, join with 1 ss into first dc.

2nd row 1 dc into same place as last ss, 2 ch, 1 ss into turning ch at base (to the right) of any section of cross, 2 ch, 1 dc into each of next 2 dc on ring, 2 ch, miss next 5 sts on section, 1 ss into next st, 2 ch, 1 dc into each of next 2 dc on ring, 4 ch, 1 dc into each of next 2 dc on ring, 2 ch, miss next 5 sts on section, 1 ss into next st, 2 ch, 1 dc into each of next 2 dc on ring, 2 ch, 1 ss into turning ch at base of section, 2 ch, (1 dc into each of next

2 dc on ring, 4 ch) 7 times, 1 dc into next dc, 1 ss into first dc (12 loops). Fasten off. Make 3 more small rings joining to base of remaining 3 sections of cross. Diagonal cross completed.

Make 4 more sections to form a cross. Make a small ring joining to base of any section as before and joining 10th and 11th loops to corresponding 2 loops of small ring on first diagonal cross.

Make and join another small ring to next section adjacent to first diagonal cross, joining corresponding loops as before.

Make and join 2 remaining small rings to complete cross.

Make 3 rows of 4 diagonal crosses joining adjacent small rings to corresponding loops. Where 4 small rings meet there should be one free loop between each 2 loop joinings.

Fill-in motifs

1st row Wind Mercer-Crochet round thumb 20 times, remove from thumb and work 60 dc into ring, join with 1 ss into first dc.

2nd row 6 ch, leaving the last loop of each on hook work 1 trip tr into next dc,

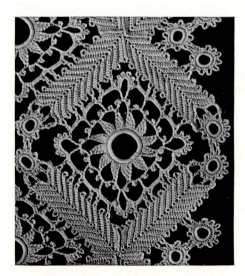

Coats ⚙ Mercer-Crochet No. 40
(20 grm).
4 balls. This model is worked in shade
503 (Coral Pink), but any other shade
of Mercer-Crochet may be used.
Milward steel crochet hook 1·00
(No. 4).

Size of diagonal cross 5 in. square.

Measurements 20 in.× 15 in.

1 dbl tr into next dc, 1 tr into next dc, 1 dc into next dc, (thread over and draw through 2 loops on hook) 4 times, ★ 5 ch, 1 dc into 5th ch from hook (picot made), 6 ch, 1 dc into 5th ch from hook (another picot made), 1 ch, leaving the last loop of each on hook work 1 quad tr into next dc, 1 trip tr into next dc, 1 dbl tr into next dc, 1 tr into next dc, 1 dc into next dc, (thread over and draw through 2 loops on hook) 5 times; repeat from ★ 10 times more, 5 ch, 1 dc into 5th ch from hook, 6 ch, 1 dc into 5th ch from hook, 1 ch, 1 ss into top of first cluster.

3rd row Ss to sp between picots, 12 ch, 1 dbl tr into same place as last ss, ★ (8 ch, 1 dbl tr into sp between next 2 picots) twice, 8 ch, into next sp between picots work 1 dbl tr 8 ch and 1 dbl tr; repeat from ★ omitting 1 dbl tr 8 ch and 1 dbl tr at end of last repeat, 1 ss into 4th of 12 ch.

4th row ★ Into next loop work (2 dc, 4 ch) 6 times and 2 dc, 2 dc into next loop, 2 ch, 1 dc into first free turning ch loop at base of dc section of cross, 2 ch, 6 dc into same loop on fill-in-motifs, 2 ch, miss one turning ch loop of cross, 1 dc into next turning ch loop, 2 ch, 2 dc into same loop on fill-in-motif, ★★ (2 dc into next loop, 2 ch, 1 dc into next turning ch loop, 2 ch, 6 dc into same loop on fill-in-motif, 2 ch, miss one turning ch loop, 1 dc into next turning ch loop, 2 ch, 2 dc into same loop on fill-in-motif) twice, ★★ into next loop work (2 dc, 4 ch) 6 times and 2 dc, 2 dc into next loop, 2 ch, miss 3 turning ch loops, 1 dc into next turning ch loop, 2 ch, 6 dc into same loop on fill-in-motif, 2 ch, miss one turning ch loop, 1 dc into next turning ch loop, 2 ch, 2 dc into same loop on fill-in-motif ★; repeat from ★★ to ★★ once and from ★ to ★ once, then from ★★ to ★★ once more, 1 ss into first dc. Fasten off. Fill in all spaces in crosses in same manner.

Outer fillings
Make necessary number of small rings and join between sections of crosses on outside edge arranging 3 small rings on each section following 'close-up' for position of joining.

Damp and pin out to measurements.

Long John runner

Long John runner

Coats 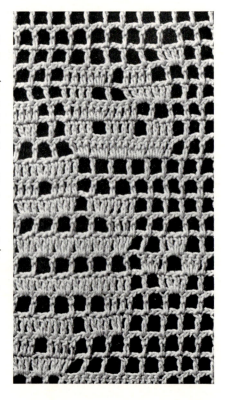 Mercer-Crochet No. 20 (20 grm).
5 balls. This model is worked in shade 521 (Jade), but any other shade of Mercer-Crochet may be used. Milward steel crochet hook 1·25 (No. 3).

Tension 5 sps and 5 rows = 1 in.

Measurements 36½ in. × 12½ in. approx.

Commence with 192 ch.

1st row 1 tr into 4th ch from hook, 1 tr into each of next 188 ch, (63 blks made), 3 ch, turn.

2nd row Miss first tr, 1 tr into each of next 3 tr (blk made at beginning of row), (2 ch, miss 2 tr, 1 tr into next tr) 61 times (61 sps made over 61 blks), 1 tr into each of next 2 tr, 1 tr into top of turning ch (blk made at end of row), 3 ch, turn.

3rd row 1 blk, (2 ch, 1 tr into next tr) 61 times (61 sps made over 61 sps), 1 blk, 3 ch, turn.

4th row 1 blk, 3 sps, 2 tr into next sp, 1 tr into next tr (blk made over sp), 5 sps and continue to follow diagram to end of row.
Follow diagram from 5th to 104th row, then 39th row to top. Fasten off.

Damp and pin out to measurements.

ALTERNATIVE SUGGESTION
Cheval Runner 12½ in. × 23½ in.
3 balls No. 20.
Follow diagram from 1st row to top.

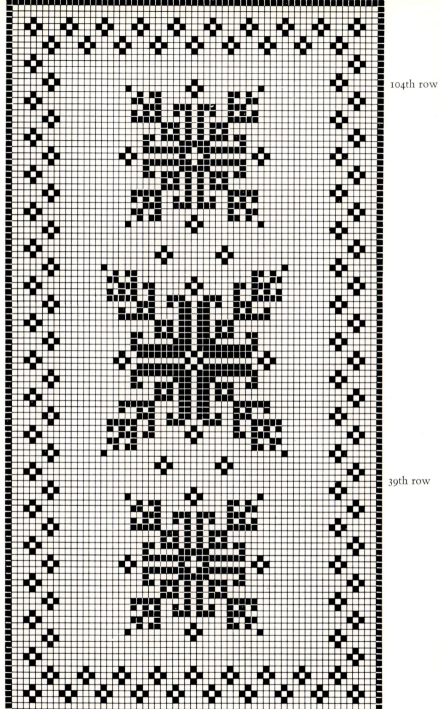

104th row

39th row

1st row

↩ Commence ch here

45

Runner

First motif

Commence with 6 ch, join with a ss to form a ring. Work over 2 strands of Mercer-Crochet.

1st row 12 dc into ring.

2nd row * 2 dc into next dc, 1 dc into next dc; repeat from * to end of row. (18 dc).

3rd row * 1 dc into each of next 2 dc, 2 dc into next dc; repeat from * to end of row. (24 dc).

4th row 1 dc into next dc, * 2 dc into next dc, 1 dc into each of next 3 dc; repeat from * ending with 2 dc into next dc, 1 dc into each of next 2 dc. (30 dc).

5th row 1 dc into each dc increasing 2 dc in row, 1 ss into back loop of first dc. (32 dc). (Cut off cording thread).

6th row 4 ch, * 1 tr into back loop of next dc, 1 ch; repeat from * ending with 1 ss into 3rd of 4 ch. (32 sps).

7th row 2 dc into each 1 ch sp, 1 ss into first dc. (64 dc).

8th row 5 ch, * miss 1 dc, 1 tr into next dc, 2 ch; repeat from * ending with 1 ss into 3rd of 5 ch. (32 sps).

9th row 3 dc into each 2 ch sp, 1 ss into back loop of first dc. (96 dc).

10th row 1 dc into same place as last ss, 1 dc into back loop of each dc, 1 ss into first dc.

11th row 1 dc into same place as last ss, * 1 dc into next dc, 3 ch, 3 tr into next dc, miss 3 dc, 1 dc into next dc; repeat from * omitting 1 dc at end of last repeat, 1 ss into first dc.
Fasten off.

Second motif

Work same as first motif for 10 rows.

11th row 1 dc into same place as last ss, 1 dc into next dc, 3 ch, remove hook, insert hook into 3 ch loop at any point on first motif and draw loop through, 3 tr into next dc on second motif, miss 3 dc, 1 dc into each of next 2 dc, 3 ch, remove hook, insert hook into 3 ch loop on next point on first motif and draw loop through, 3 tr into next dc on second motif, miss 3 dc, 1 dc into next dc and complete as for first motif.

Make 4 rows of 12 motifs joining adjacent sides as second was joined to first, leaving 2 points free on each motif between joining.

Filling

1st row Attach thread to 3 ch sp of free point after joining of motifs, 6 ch, * 1 dbl tr into 3 ch sp of next point on same motif, 2 ch, 1 dbl tr into 3 ch sp of first free point on next motif, 2 ch; repeat from * omitting 1 dbl tr and 2 ch at end of last repeat, 1 ss into 4th of 6 ch.

2nd row 2 dc into each 2 ch sp, 1 ss into first dc. Fasten off.

Fill in all spaces between motifs in same manner.

Damp and pin out to measurements.

Coats ❀ Mercer-Crochet No. 20 (20 grm).

5 balls. This model is worked in shade 463 (Parrot Green), but any other shade of Mercer-Crochet may be used.

Milward steel crochet hook 1·25 (No. 3).

Size of motif 2¾ in. in diameter.

Measurements 33 in. × 11 in.

Runner

Coats ⊙ Mercer-Crochet No. 20 (20 grm).
2 balls. This model is worked in shade 469 (Geranium), but any other shade of Mercer-Crochet may be used.
Piece of Old Bleach linen CO1 (Biscuit) 13½ in. × 48½ in.
Milward steel crochet hook 1·25 (No. 3).

Size of motifs
Large   = 3¼ in.
Medium = 2 in.
Small   = 1 in.
Measurements 12 in. × 47 in.

Large motif (make 6)

First motif
Commence with 6 ch, join with a ss to form a ring.

1st row 4 ch (to stand for one dbl tr), 1 dbl tr into ring, ★ 3 ch, 1 trip tr into ring, 3 ch, 2 dbl tr into ring; repeat from ★ twice more, 3 ch, 1 trip tr into ring, 3 ch, 1 ss into 4th of 4 ch. Fasten off.

Second motif
Commence with 6 ch, join with a ss to form a ring.

1st row 4 ch (to stand for one dbl tr), 1 dbl tr into ring, 3 ch, remove hook, insert hook into trip tr of previous motif and draw dropped loop through, 1 trip tr into ring, 3 ch, remove hook, insert hook into next dbl tr of previous motif and draw dropped loop through, 1 dbl tr into ring, remove hook, insert hook into next dbl tr of previous motif and draw dropped loop through, 1 dbl tr into ring, 3 ch, remove hook, insert hook into next trip tr of previous motif and draw dropped loop through, 1 trip

tr into ring, complete motif as before. Make and join 3 more motifs, joining one to each free side of first motif.

1st outer row Attach thread to trip tr to right of joining, 3 dc into same place as join, ★ 3 dc into next sp, 3 ch, 1 dbl tr into each of next 2 dbl tr, 3 ch, 3 dc into next sp, 3 dc into sp of next motif, 3 ch, 1 dbl tr into each of next 2 dbl tr, 3 ch, 3 dc into next sp, 3 dc into next trip tr, 3 dc into next sp, 3 ch, 1 dbl tr into each of next 2 dbl tr, 3 ch, 3 dc into next sp, 3 dc into next trip tr; repeat from ★ omitting 3 dc at end of last repeat, 1 ss into first dc.

2nd outer row 1 dc into next dc, 8 ch, 1 dc into 3rd of next 3 ch, ★ 8 ch, miss next 2 dbl tr 3 ch 6 dc 3 ch and 2 dbl tr, 1 dc into first of next 3 ch, 8 ch, miss next 4 dc, 1 dc into next dc, 8 ch, 1 dc into 3rd of next 3 ch, 9 ch, 1 dc into first of next 3 ch, 8 ch, miss 4 dc, 1 dc into next dc, 8 ch, 1 dc into 3rd of next 3 ch; repeat from ★ omitting 1 dc 8 ch and 1 dc at end of last repeat, 1 ss into first dc.

3rd outer row 1 ss into first loop, 3 ch, ★ 2 tr 3 ch and 2 tr into same loop, (leaving the last loop of each on hook work 1 tr into same loop and 1 tr into next loop, thread over and draw through all loops on hook—a joint tr made, 2 tr 3 ch and 2 tr into same loop as last tr) 3 times. Work a joint tr as before, 2 tr 3 ch 3 tr 3 ch and 2 tr into same (corner loop). Work a joint tr as before, 2 tr 3 ch and 2 tr into same loop as last tr, work a joint tr as before; repeat from ★ omitting 1 tr at end of last repeat, 1 ss into 3rd of 3 ch. Fasten off.

Medium motif (make 5)
Work same as large motif until 1st outer row has been completed. Fasten off.

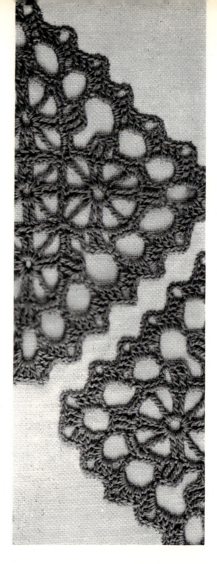

Small motif (make 6)
Work first motif as before.

1st outer row Attach thread to first trip tr, 3 dc into same trip tr, ★ 3 dc into next sp, 3 ch, 1 dbl tr into each of next 2 dbl tr, 3 ch, 3 dc into next sp, 3 dc into next trip tr; repeat from ★ omitting 3 dc at end of last repeat, 1 ss into first dc. Fasten off.

Starch and pin out motifs to measurements.

To make up
Make $\frac{1}{2}$ in. hems all round linen.

Make the centre lengthwise and widthwise on linen with a line of basting stitches. The diagram gives a little more than one half of design, the exact centre lines are marked by broken lines. Place one medium motif in exact centre and arrange other 2 medium 3 large and 3 small motifs spaced as shown on diagram. Work the other half to correspond. Sew neatly in place.

Damp and press.

3¾″

⅛″

Star ruffle doily

Star ruffle doily

Coats ❀ Mercer-Crochet No. 40 (20 grm).

3 balls. This model is worked in shade 693 (Carnation Pink), but any other shade of Mercer-Crochet may be used.

Milward steel crochet hook 1·00 (No. 4).

Tension First 2 rows = $1\frac{1}{4}$ in. in diameter.

Measurement $16\frac{1}{2}$ in. in diameter (including ruffle).

Commence with 9 ch, join with a ss to form a ring.

1st row 9 ch, (1 dbl tr into ring, 5 ch) 5 times, 1 ss into 4th of 9 ch.

2nd row 1 ss into next sp, 4 ch, 6 dbl tr into same sp, * 5 ch, 7 dbl tr into next sp; repeat from * ending with 5 ch, 1 ss into 4th of 4 ch.

3rd row 4 ch, 1 dbl tr into each of next 6 dbl tr, * 5 ch, 1 dbl tr into next sp, 5 ch, 1 dbl tr into each of next 7 dbl tr; repeat from * ending with 5 ch, 1 dbl tr into next sp, 5 ch, 1 ss into 4th of 4 ch.

4th row 4 ch, 1 dbl tr into each of next 6 dbl tr, * (5 ch, 1 dbl tr into next sp) twice, 5 ch, 1 dbl tr into each of next 7 dbl tr; repeat from * ending with (5 ch, 1 dbl tr into next sp) twice, 5 ch, 1 ss into 4th of 4 ch.

5th to 10th row Work as for 4th row having one sp more between dbl tr groups on each row.

11th row 9 ch, * miss next dbl tr group, 7 dbl tr into next sp, (5 ch, 1 dbl tr into next sp) 7 times, 5 ch, 7 dbl tr into next sp, 5 ch; repeat from * ending with 6 dbl tr into last sp, 1 ss into 4th of 9 ch.

12th row 1 ss into each of next 3 ch, 9 ch, * 7 dbl tr into next sp, (5 ch, 1 dbl tr into next sp) 6 times, 5 ch, 7 dbl tr into next sp, 5 ch, 1 dbl tr into next sp, 5 ch; repeat from * omitting 5 ch, 1 dbl tr and 5 ch at end of last repeat, ending with 2 ch, 1 tr into 4th of 9 ch.

13th row 9 ch, 1 dbl tr into next sp, * 5 ch, 7 dbl tr into next sp, (5 ch, 1 dbl tr into next sp) 5 times, 5 ch, 7 dbl tr into next sp, (5 ch, 1 dbl tr into next sp) twice; repeat from * omitting 5 ch 1 dbl tr and 5 ch at end of last repeat, ending with 2 ch, 1 tr into 4th of 9 ch.

14th row 10 ch, (1 dbl tr into next sp, 6 ch) twice, * 7 dbl tr into next sp, (5 ch, 1 dbl tr into next sp) 4 times, 5 ch, 7 dbl tr into next sp, (6 ch, 1 dbl tr into next sp) 3 times, 6 ch; repeat from * omitting (6 ch, 1 dbl tr into next sp) 3 times and 6 ch at end of last repeat, ending with 3 ch, 1 tr into 4th of 10 ch.

15th row 11 ch, (1 dbl tr into next sp, 7 ch) 3 times, * 7 dbl tr into next sp, (5 ch, 1 dbl tr into next sp) 3 times, 5 ch, 7 dbl tr into next sp, (7 ch, 1 dbl tr into next sp) 4 times, 7 ch; repeat from * omitting (7 ch, 1 dbl tr into next sp) 4 times and 7 ch at end of last repeat, ending with 3 ch, 1 dbl tr into 4th of 11 ch.

16th row 12 ch, (1 dbl tr into next sp, 8 ch) 4 times, * 7 dbl tr into next sp, (5 ch, 1 dbl tr into next sp) twice, 5 ch, 7 dbl tr into next sp, (8 ch, 1 dbl tr into next sp) 5 times, 8 ch; repeat from * omitting (8 ch, 1 dbl tr into next sp) 5 times and 8 ch at end of last repeat, ending with 4 ch, 1 dbl tr into 4th of 12 ch.

17th row 12 ch, (1 dbl tr into next sp, 8 ch) 5 times, * 7 dbl tr into next sp, 5 ch, 1 dbl tr into next sp, 5 ch, 7 dbl tr into next sp, (8 ch, 1 dbl tr into next sp) 6 times, 8 ch; repeat from * omitting (8 ch, 1 dbl tr into next sp) 6 times and 8 ch at end of last repeat, ending with 4 ch, 1 dbl tr into 4th of 12 ch.

18th row 13 ch, (1 dbl tr into next sp, 9 ch) 6 times, ★ 7 dbl tr into next sp, 5 ch, 7 dbl tr into next sp, (9 ch, 1 dbl tr into next sp) 7 times, 9 ch; repeat from ★ ending with 7 dbl tr into next sp, 5 ch, 7 dbl tr into next sp, 4 ch, 1 trip tr into 4th of 13 ch.

19th row 13 ch, (1 dbl tr into next sp, 9 ch) 7 times, ★ 7 dbl tr into next sp, (9 ch, 1 dbl tr into next sp) 8 times, 9 ch; repeat from ★ ending with 7 dbl tr into next sp, 4 ch, 1 trip tr into 4th of 13 ch.

20th row 14 ch, (1 dbl tr into next sp, 10 ch) 8 times, ★ miss 3 dbl tr of next dbl tr group, 1 dbl tr into next dbl tr, (10 ch, 1 dbl tr into next sp) 9 times, 10 ch; repeat from ★ omitting 10 ch at end of last repeat, ending with 4 ch, 1 trip tr into 5th of 14 ch.

21st row 15 ch, ★ 1 dbl tr into next sp, 11 ch; repeat from ★ ending with 1 ss into 4th of 15 ch.

22nd row 15 dc into each sp, 1 ss into first dc.

Ruffle

1st row ★ 7 ch, 1 dc into next dc; repeat from ★ ending with 7 ch, 1 ss into first dc.

2nd and 3rd rows Ss to centre of next loop, 9 ch, ★ 1 dbl tr into next loop, 5 ch; repeat from ★ ending with 1 ss into 4th of 9 ch.

4th to 6th row Ss to centre of next sp, 11 ch, ★ 1 dbl tr into next sp, 7 ch; repeat from ★ ending with 1 ss into 4th of 11 ch. Fasten off.

Starch, pin out to measurement, pull ruffle into shape and leave to dry.

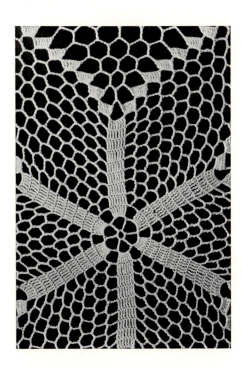

Lacis chairback

Coats ⚛ Mercer-Crochet No. 20 (20 grm).

3 balls. This model is worked in shade Spec. 8918 (Lt Coral Pink), but any other shade of Mercer-Crochet may be used.

Milward steel crochet hook 1·25 (No. 3).

Tension 3 sps and 3 rows = 1 in.

Measurements 13½ in. × 23 in. approx.

Commence with 167 ch.

1st row 1 dbl tr into 11th ch from hook, (3 ch, miss 3 ch, 1 dbl tr into next ch) 39 times (40 sps made), 7 ch, turn.

2nd row Miss first dbl tr, 1 dbl tr into next dbl tr (sp made over sp), leaving the last loop of each on hook work 3 dbl tr into next dbl tr, thread over and draw through all loops on hook (a 3 dbl tr cluster made), (4 ch, a 2 dbl tr cluster into 4th ch from hook) twice, a 3 dbl tr cluster into same place as last 3 dbl tr cluster (diamond cluster made), ★ 1 dbl tr into next dbl tr, (3 ch, 1 dbl tr into next dbl tr) twice, (2 sps made over 2 sps), a diamond cluster into next dbl tr; repeat from ★ ending with 1 dbl tr into next dbl tr, 3 ch, miss 3 ch, 1 dbl tr into next ch (sp made at end of row), 7 ch, turn.

3rd row 1 sp, ★ 3 ch, 1 dc into centre of diamond, 3 ch, 1 dbl tr into next dbl tr, 2 sps; repeat from ★ omitting 1 sp at end of last repeat, 7 ch, turn.

Continue to follow diagram for 2 rows.

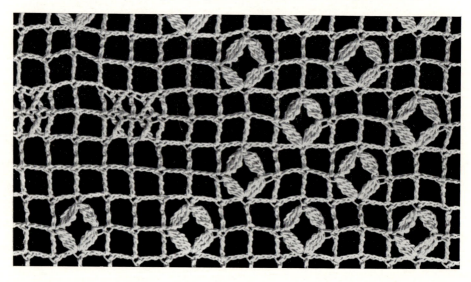

6th row 1 sp, (a diamond cluster into next dbl tr, 1 dbl tr into next dbl tr, 2 sps) twice, (2 sps, miss 2 sts, 1 dbl tr into next st, 1 ch, inserting hook from behind last dbl tr work 1 dbl tr into first of 2 sts missed—a cross made—1 dbl tr into next dbl tr, 1 cross, 1 dbl tr into next dbl tr) 5 times, 4 sps and continue to follow diagram to end of row, 7 ch, turn.

7th to 11th row Follow diagram.
Repeat 4th to 7th row (section within brackets) 11 times more, 4th and 5th rows once more, then 2nd row to top. Fasten off.

Edging

With right side facing, attach thread to any sp on first row and work a row of dc all round having 5 dc into each sp and 11 dc into each corner sp, 1 ss into first dc. Fasten off.

Damp and pin out to measurements.

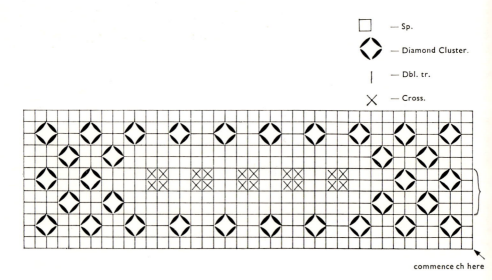

□ — Sp.

◇ — Diamond Cluster.

| — Dbl. tr.

X — Cross.

commence ch here

56

Coats ⊕ Mercer-Crochet No. 20 (20 grm).

3 balls. This model is worked in shade 442 (Mid Buttercup), but any other shade of Mercer-Crochet may be used.

Milward steel crochet hook 1·25 (No. 3).

Pineapple chairback

Tension Depth of complete pineapple = $2\frac{3}{8}$ in. approx.

Measurements $12\frac{1}{2}$ in. × 18 in. approx.

Pineapple chairback

Commence at top with 249 ch to measure 20 in.

1st row 1 dc into 2nd ch from hook, 3 ch, ★ 1 dc into next ch, 5 ch, miss 7 ch, 5 tr into next ch (shell made), (miss 2 ch, 1 dc into next ch, miss 2 ch, shell into next ch) 4 times, 5 ch, miss 7 ch, 1 dc into next ch, 5 ch; repeat from ★ 5 times more, having 3 ch instead of 5 ch at end of last repeat, 1 dc into next ch, turn.

2nd row 1 ss into first dc, 4 ch, 2 tr into first 3 ch loop, ★ 5 ch, (1 dc into centre tr of next shell, 1 shell into next dc) 4 times, 1 dc into centre tr of next shell, 5 ch, miss next 5 ch sp, shell into next 5 ch loop; repeat from ★ ending with 5 ch, (1 dc into centre tr of next shell, 1 shell into next dc) 4 times, 1 dc into centre tr of next shell, 5 ch, miss 5 ch, 2 tr into last 3 ch loop, 1 ch, 1 tr into last dc, 5 ch, turn.

3rd row Miss first tr, 3 tr into next 1 ch sp, ★ 5 ch, (1 dc into centre tr of next shell, shell into next dc) 3 times, 1 dc into centre tr of next shell, 5 ch, into centre tr of next shell work 3 tr 3 ch and 3 tr; repeat from ★ to within last 5 ch sp, 5 ch, miss next 5 ch sp and 2 tr, 3 tr into next sp, 1 ch, 1 dbl tr into 3rd of turning ch, 1 ch, turn.

4th row 1 dc into first dbl tr, ★ 3 ch, miss next tr, shell into next tr, 5 ch, (1 dc into next shell, shell into next dc) twice, 1 dc into next shell, 5 ch, miss next 5 ch sp and next tr, shell into next tr, 3 ch, 1 dc into next 3 ch sp; repeat from ★ ending with 1 dc into 4th of turning ch, 3 ch, turn.

5th row 1 dc into next 3 ch sp, ★ 3 ch, shell into centre tr of next shell, (shell made over shell), 5 ch, 1 dc into next shell, shell into next dc, 1 dc into next shell, 5 ch, shell over shell, (3 ch, 1 dc into next 3 ch loop) twice; repeat from ★ ending with 1 dc into last 3 ch sp, 1 ch, 1 dc into last dc, 4 ch, turn.

6th row 4 dbl tr into next 1 ch sp, ★ 3 ch, shell over shell, 5 ch, into centre tr of next shell work (1 dc, 10 ch) 5 times and 1 dc, 5 ch, shell over shell, 3 ch, miss next 3 ch sp, 9 dbl tr into next 3 ch sp; repeat from ★ ending with 3 ch, 5 dbl tr into last sp, 5 ch, turn.

7th row Miss first dbl tr, (1 dbl tr into next dbl tr, 1 ch) 3 times, 1 dbl tr into next dbl tr, ★ shell over shell, (1 dc into next 10 ch loop, 3 ch) 4 times, 1 dc into next 10 ch loop, shell over shell, (1 dbl tr into next dbl tr, 1 ch) 8 times, 1 dbl tr into next dbl tr; repeat from ★ ending with (1 dbl tr into next dbl tr, 1 ch) 4 times, 1 dbl tr into top of turning ch, 3 ch, turn.

8th row 2 tr into first dbl tr (half shell made), (1 dc into next dbl tr, shell into next dbl tr) twice, ★ 5 ch, miss next shell and next 3 ch sp, (1 dc into next 3 ch sp, 5 ch) twice, (shell into next dbl tr, 1 dc into next dbl tr) 4 times, shell into next dbl tr; repeat from ★ to within last 4 dbl tr, (shell into next dbl tr, 1 dc into next dbl tr) twice, 3 tr into 4th of turning ch (another half shell made), 1 ch, turn.

9th row 1 dc into first tr, (shell into next dc, 1 dc into next shell) twice, ★ 5 ch, miss next 5 ch sp, shell into next 5 ch sp, 5 ch, (1 dc into next shell, shell into next dc) 4 times, 1 dc into next shell; repeat from ★ ending with 1 dc into top of turning ch, 3 ch, turn.

10th row 1 half shell into first dc, 1 dc into next shell, shell into next dc, 1 dc into next shell, ★ 5 ch, into centre tr of next shell work 3 tr 3 ch and 3 tr, 5 ch, (1 dc into next shell, shell into next dc) 3 times, 1 dc into next shell; repeat from ★ ending with 1 half shell into last dc, 1 ch, turn.

11th row 1 dc into first tr, shell into next dc, 1 dc into next shell, ★ 5 ch, miss next 5 ch sp and next tr, shell into next tr, 3 ch,

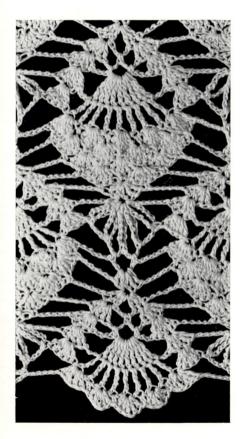

1 dc into next sp, 3 ch, miss next tr, shell into next tr, 5 ch, (1 dc into next shell, shell into next dc) twice, 1 dc into next shell; repeat from * ending with 1 dc into top of turning ch, 3 ch, turn.

12th row 1 half shell into first dc, * 1 dc into next shell, 5 ch, shell over shell, (3 ch, 1 dc into next 3 ch sp) twice, 3 ch, shell over shell, 5 ch, 1 dc into next shell, 1 shell into next dc; repeat from * ending with 1 dc into last shell, 1 half shell into next dc, 10 ch, turn.

13th row (1 dc into first tr, 10 ch) twice, 1 dc into same tr, * 5 ch, miss next 5 ch sp, shell over shell, 3 ch, miss next 3 ch sp, 9 dbl tr into next 3 ch sp, 3 ch, miss next 3 ch sp, shell over shell, 5 ch, into centre tr of next shell work (1 dc, 10 ch) 5 times and 1 dc; repeat from * ending with (1 dc, 10 ch) twice and 1 dc into top of turning ch, 5 ch, 1 trip tr into same place as last dc, 1 ch, turn.

14th row Miss trip tr, 1 dc into 5 ch loop, (3 ch, 1 dc into next 10 ch loop) twice, * shell over shell, (1 dbl tr into next dbl tr, 1 ch) 8 times, 1 dbl tr into next dbl tr, shell over shell, 1 dc into next 10 ch loop, (3 ch, 1 dc into next 10 ch loop) 4 times; repeat from * ending last repeat with (3 ch, 1 dc into next 10 ch loop) twice, 1 ch, turn.

15th row 1 dc into first dc, 3 ch, 1 dc into first 3 ch sp, * 5 ch, miss next 3 ch sp and next shell, (shell into next dbl tr, 1 dc into next dbl tr) 4 times, shell into next dbl tr, 5 ch, miss next shell and next 3 ch sp, 1 dc into next 3 ch sp, 5 ch, 1 dc into next 3 ch sp; repeat from * ending with 1 dc into last 3 ch sp, 3 ch, 1 dc into next dc, turn.

Repeat 2nd to 15th row inclusive until 57 rows have been completed, then work 2nd to 8th row. Fasten off.

Damp and pin out to measurements.

59

Square motif chairback

First motif

Commence with 10 ch, join with a ss to form a ring.

1st row 4 ch, into ring work (1 tr, 1 ch) 15 times, 1 ss into 3rd of 4 ch.

2nd row 11 ch, (miss 1 tr, 1 quad tr into next tr, 7 ch, miss 1 tr, 1 dbl tr into next tr, 7 ch) 3 times, miss 1 tr, 1 quad tr into next tr, 7 ch, 1 ss into 4th of 11 ch.

3rd row ★ 7 ch, miss 3 ch, 1 ss into next st; repeat from ★ ending with 3 ch, 1 dbl tr into ss of previous row.

4th row ★ (9 ch, 1 ss into 4th ch of next loop) twice, 9 ch, 1 tr into next ss, 11 ch, 1 ss into top of last tr, (9 ch, 1 ss into 4th ch of next loop) twice; repeat from ★ omitting 9 ch and 1 ss at end of last repeat, 4 ch, 1 trip tr into dbl tr at end of previous row.

5th row 7 ch, 1 quad tr into top of trip tr, ★ 1 ch, leaving the last loop of each on hook work 1 quad tr into same place and 1 quad tr into centre ch of next loop, thread over and draw through all loops on hook (a joint quad tr made), 1 ch, 1 quad tr into same place as last quad tr; repeat from ★ once more, 1 ch, 1 joint quad tr as before, (1 ch, 1 quad tr into same place as last quad tr) 3 times, 1 ch, 1 joint quad tr as before, into same place as last quad tr work (1 ch, 1 quad tr) twice, 1 ch, 1 quin tr and (1 ch, 1 quad tr) twice, 1 ch, 1 joint quad tr as before, (1 ch, 1 quad tr into same place as last quad tr) 3 times, 1 ch, 1 joint quad tr as before, 1 ch, 1 quad tr into same place as last quad tr; repeat from first ★ omitting 1 joint quad tr 1 ch and 1 quad tr at end of last repeat, leaving the last 2 loops on hook, work 1 quad tr into same place as last quad tr, 1 ss into 6th of 7 ch drawing through all loops on hook.

6th row 1 dc into same place as last ss, ★ (7 ch, miss 1 quad tr, 1 dc into next joint quad tr) 3 times, 7 ch, miss 1 quad tr, 1 dc into next quad tr, 7 ch, miss 1 quad tr, 1 dc into next joint quad tr, 7 ch, miss 1 quad tr, 1 dc into next quad tr, 7 ch, into next quin tr work 1 dc 9 ch and 1 dc, 7 ch, 1 dc into next quad tr, 7 ch, miss 1 quad tr, 1 dc into next joint quad tr, 7 ch, miss 1 quad tr, 1 dc into next quad tr, 7 ch, miss 1 quad tr, 1 dc into next joint quad tr; repeat from ★ omitting 1 dc at end of last repeat, 1 ss into first dc. Fasten off.

Second motif

Work same as first motif for 5 rows.

6th row 1 dc into same place as last ss, (7 ch, miss 1 quad tr, 1 dc into next joint quad tr) 3 times, 7 ch, miss 1 quad tr, 1 dc into next quad tr, 7 ch, miss 1 quad tr, 1 dc into next joint quad tr, 7 ch, miss 1 quad tr, 1 dc into next quad tr, 7 ch, 1 dc into next quin tr, 4 ch, 1 ss into corresponding loop on first motif, 4 ch, 1 dc into same quin tr on second motif, 3 ch, 1 ss into next 7 ch loop on first motif, 3 ch, 1 dc into next quad tr on second motif, 3 ch, 1 ss into next 7 ch loop on first motif, 3 ch, miss 1 quad tr, 1 dc into next joint quad tr on second motif, 3 ch, 1 ss into next 7 ch loop on first motif, 3 ch, miss 1 quad tr, 1 dc into next quad tr on second motif, (3 ch, 1 ss into next 7 ch loop on first motif, 3 ch, miss 1 quad tr, 1 dc into next joint quad tr on second motif) 4 times, 3 ch, 1 ss into next 7 ch loop on first motif, 3 ch, miss 1 quad tr, 1 dc into next quad tr on second motif, 3 ch, 1 ss into next 7 ch loop on first motif, 3 ch, miss 1 quad tr, 1 dc into next joint quad tr on second motif, 3 ch, 1 ss into next 7 ch loop on first motif, 3 ch, miss 1 quad tr, 1 dc into next quad tr on second motif, 3 ch, 1 ss into next 7 ch loop on first motif, 3 ch, 1 dc into next quin tr on second motif, 4 ch, 1 ss into next 9 ch loop

on first motif, 4 ch, 1 dc into same quin tr on second motif and complete as for first motif. Make 7 rows of 5 motifs joining adjacent sides as second was joined to first (where 4 corners meet, join 3rd and 4th motifs to ss at joining of first 2 motifs).

Damp and pin out to measurements.

Coats ⚙ **Mercer-Crochet No. 40 (20 grm).**
3 balls. This model is worked in shade 521 (Jade), but any other shade of Mercer-Crochet may be used.
Milward steel crochet hook 1·00 (No. 4).
Size of motif $3\frac{1}{4}$ in.
Measurements $16\frac{1}{4}$ in. $\times$ $22\frac{3}{4}$ in. (5 motifs $\times$ 7 motifs).

Settee back, chair-back and armrest

Settee back

First motif

Wind thread round middle finger 6 times and slip off finger.

1st row Into ring just made work 32 dc.

2nd and 3rd rows 1 dc into each dc, ending last row with 1 ss into first dc.

4th row 1 dc into same place as last ss, ★ 13 ch, miss 7 dc, 1 dc into next dc; repeat from ★ twice more, 13 ch, miss 7 dc, 1 ss into first dc.

5th row Into each loop work (3 dc, 5 ch) 5 times and 3 dc, 1 ss into first dc. Fasten off.

Second motif

Work same as first motif for 4 rows.

5th row Into next loop work (3 dc, 5 ch) 3 times and 3 dc, 2 ch, 1 ss into corresponding 5 ch loop on first motif, 2 ch, 3 dc into same loop on second motif, 2 ch, 1 ss into next 5 ch loop on first motif, 2 ch, 3 dc into same loop on second motif, 3 dc into next loop, 2 ch, 1 ss into first 5 ch loop on next loop on first motif, 2 ch, 3 dc into same loop on second motif, 2 ch, 1 ss into next 5 ch loop on first motif, 2 ch, 3 dc into same loop on second motif, (5 ch, 3 dc into same loop) 3 times and complete as for first motif.

Make 13 rows of 7 motifs joining adjacent sides as second motif was joined to first motif.

Edging

1st row Attach thread to 2nd free loop to left of joining of first 2 motifs on long side, 1 dc into same place as join, ★ (3 ch, 1 dc into next loop of same motif) 3 times, 7 ch, 1 dc into 2nd free loop of next motif; repeat from ★ to next corner motif, (3 ch, 1 dc into next loop) 3 times, 9 ch, miss 1 loop, 1 dc into next loop, (3 ch, 1 dc into next loop) 3 times, 7 ch, 1 dc into 2nd free loop of next motif; repeat from first ★ all round, omitting 1 dc at end of last repeat, 1 ss into first dc.

2nd row 3 ch, 1 tr into each st working 3 tr into centre ch at corners, 1 ss into 3rd of 3 ch. Fasten off.

3rd row Commence with 6 ch, 1 dc into centre tr at corner, ★ 7 ch, 1 dc into 2nd ch from hook, 1 dc into each of next 12 sts, 1 ch, turn, ★ 1 dc into each dc, 1 ch, turn; repeat from last ★ twice more, omitting turning ch at end of last repeat, ss along row-ends, ★ 6 ch, miss 5 tr, 1 dc into next tr, turn, 1 dc into each of next 6 ch, 1 ch, turn, (1 dc into each dc, 1 ch, turn) 3 times omitting turning ch at end of last repeat (block made); repeat from last ★ twice more, ★ 6 ch, miss 7 tr, 1 dc into next tr and complete a block as before, (6 ch, miss 5 tr, 1 dc into next tr and complete a block as before) twice; repeat from last ★ to corner, 6 ch, miss 5 tr, 1 dc into centre tr at corner; repeat from first ★ all round omitting 6 ch and 1 dc at end of last repeat and joining last dc to first ch made. Fasten off.

4th row Attach thread to centre dc of any corner block, 9 ch, miss 5 dc, 1 dc into next dc, ★ 6 ch, 1 dc into first dc of last row of small block; repeat from ★ to next corner, 6 ch, miss 5 dc, 1 tr into next dc, 6 ch, miss 5 dc, 1 dc into next dc; repeat from first ★ omitting 1 tr 6 ch and 1 dc at end of last repeat, 1 ss into 3rd of 9 ch.

5th row 3 ch, 1 tr into each st, 1 ss into 3rd of 3 ch.

6th row 1 dc into same place as last ss, ★ 7 ch, miss 6 tr, 1 dc into next tr; repeat from ★ omitting 1 dc at end of last repeat, 1 ss into first dc.

Furniture and accessories by Overgard

Coats ✿ Mercer-Crochet No. 20 (20 grm).
1 ball. This model is worked in shade 521 (Jade), but any other shade of Mercer-Crochet may be used.
½ yd Old Bleach linen L582 (Wedgewood).
Milward steel crochet hook 1·25 (No. 3).

Size of motifs
Large   4 in. square.
Medium   3¼ in. from point to point.
Small   1¼ in. square.
Measurement 16 in. square.

Cushion

Cushion

Large motif (make 4)

Commence with 17 ch.

1st row 1 dbl tr into 5th ch from hook, 4 ch, miss 4 ch, 1 dbl tr into each of next 2 ch, 4 ch, miss 4 ch, 1 dbl tr into each of next 2 ch, 1 ch, turn.

2nd row 1 dc into each of first 2 dbl tr, 4 dc into next sp, 1 dc into each of next 2 dbl tr, 4 dc into next sp, 1 dc into next dbl tr, 1 dc into top of 4 ch, 4 ch, turn.

3rd row Miss first dc, 1 dbl tr into next dc, (4 ch, miss 4 dc, 1 dbl tr into each of next 2 dc) twice, 1 ch, turn.

4th row As 2nd row, turning with 15 ch.

5th row 1 dbl tr into 5th ch from hook, 4 ch, miss 4 ch, 1 dbl tr into each of next 2 ch, 4 ch, miss 4 ch, 1 dbl tr into each of next 2 dc, (4 ch, miss 4 dc, 1 dbl tr into each of next 2 dc) twice, 8 ch, 1 dbl tr into same place as last dbl tr, 4 ch, turn, 1 ss into 4th of 8 ch, 8 ch, turn, 1 dbl tr into 1st of 4 ch, 4 ch, turn, 1 ss into 4th of 8 ch.

6th row 2 dc into same place as last ss, 4 dc into next sp, 1 dc into top of next 4 ch, 1 dc into same place as ss, (4 dc into next sp, 1 dc into each of next 2 dbl tr) 4 times, 4 dc into next sp, 1 dc into next dbl tr, 1 dc into top of turning ch, 4 ch, turn.

7th row Miss first dc, 1 dbl tr into next dc, (4 ch, miss 4 dc, 1 dbl tr into each of next 2 dc) 6 times, 1 ch, turn.

8th row 1 ss into each of first 12 sts, 1 dc into each of next 2 dbl tr, (4 dc into next sp, 1 dc into each of next 2 dbl tr) twice, 4 ch, turn.

9th row As 3rd row.

10th row As 2nd row.

11th and 12th rows As 3rd and 2nd rows, omitting turning ch on last row.

13th row 4 ch, 1 dbl tr over turning ch at beginning of 11th row, 1 dbl tr into side of next dc, 1 dbl tr into top of next ch, 1 dbl tr over turning ch, 1 dbl tr into next 4 ch sp, 1 dbl tr into each of next 2 dbl tr, 1 dbl tr into next sp, 4 ch, 1 dc into top of turning ch, 4 ch, 1 dbl tr over next row-end, 1 dbl tr into side of next dc, 1 dbl tr into top of turning ch, 1 dbl tr over next row-end, 4 ch, 1 dc into base of same row-end, 4 ch, 1 dbl tr into next sp, 1 dbl tr into ch at base of each of next 2 dbl tr, 1 dbl tr into next sp, 1 dbl tr over next turning ch, 1 dbl tr into side of next dc, 1 dbl tr into top of turning ch, 1 dbl tr over next row-end, 4 ch, 1 dc into base of same row-end, 4 ch, 1 dbl tr into next sp, 1 dbl tr into ch at base of next 2 dbl tr, 1 dbl tr into next sp, 4 ch, 1 dc into first of foundation ch, 4 ch, 1 dbl tr over next row-end, 1 dbl tr into top of next dbl tr, 1 dbl tr into side of next dc, 1 dbl tr over next row-end, 1 dbl tr into next sp, 1 dbl tr into ch at base of next 2 dbl tr, 1 dbl tr into next sp, 4 ch, 1 dc at base of turning ch, 4 ch, 1 dbl tr over next row-end, 1 dbl tr at side of next dc, 1 dbl tr into base of next dbl tr, 1 dbl tr over next row-end, 4 ch, 1 dc into top of same dbl tr, 4 ch, 1 dbl tr into next sp, 1 dbl tr into each of next 2 dbl tr, 1 dbl tr into next sp, 1 dbl tr over next row-end, 1 dbl tr into top of dbl tr, 1 dbl tr into side of next dc, 1 dbl tr over next row-end, 4 ch, 1 dc into first dc of 12th row, 4 ch, miss 4 dc, 1 dbl tr into each of next 4 dc, 4 ch, 1 ss into last dc on 12th row.

14th row 1 ss into each of next 2 ch, 1 dc into sp, * 11 ch, 1 dc into next 4 ch sp, (7 ch, 1 dc into next 4 ch sp) 3 times; repeat from * omitting 1 dc at end of last repeat, 1 ss into first dc.

15th row 1 ss into each of next 2 ch, 1 dc into 11 ch loop, ★ 7 ch, 1 dc into same loop, (7 ch, 1 dc into next loop) twice, 9 ch, 1 dc into same loop at corner, (7 ch, 1 dc into next loop) twice; repeat from ★ omitting 1 dc at end of last repeat, 1 ss into first dc.

16th row 1 ss into loop, 3 ch, 2 tr 3 ch and 3 tr into same loop, ★ 3 tr 3 ch and 3 tr into each of next 2 loops, into corner loop work 3 tr 3 ch 3 tr 3 ch 3 tr 3 ch and 3 tr, 3 tr 3 ch and 3 tr into each of next 3 loops; repeat from ★ omitting 3 tr 3 ch and 3 tr at end of last repeat, 1 ss into 3rd of 3 ch. Fasten off.

Medium motif (make 1)

Work same as large motif for 13 rows. Fasten off.

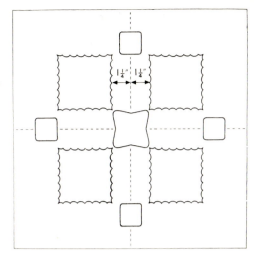

Small motif (make 4)

Work same as large motif for 3 rows.

4th row 1 dc into first dbl tr, 4 ch, 1 dbl tr into next sp, 1 dbl tr into each of next 2 dbl tr, 1 dbl tr into next sp, 4 ch, miss next dbl tr, 1 dc into top of turning ch, 4 ch, 1 dbl tr over turning ch, 1 dbl tr into side of next dc, 1 dbl tr into top

of next row-end, 1 dbl tr over next row-end, 4 ch, 1 dc into ch at base of same row-end, 4 ch, 1 dbl tr into next sp, 1 dbl tr into ch at base of each of next 2 dbl tr, 1 dbl tr into next sp, 4 ch, 1 dc into first of foundation ch, 4 ch, 1 dbl tr over next row-end, 1 dbl tr into top of same row-end, 1 dbl tr into side of next dc, 1 dbl tr over next row-end, 4 ch, 1 ss into first dc. Fasten off.

Starch and pin out motifs to measurements.

Cut two pieces from linen 17 in. square. Mark the centre each way on one piece with a line of basting stitches. Diagram H gives full arrangement of design, the exact centre lines are marked by broken lines. Place medium motif in exact centre and arrange 4 large and 4 small motifs spaced as shown in the diagram. Sew neatly in place.

Damp and press.

To make up Place the two sections right sides together and machine stitch round 1 in. from the edge leaving an opening on one side sufficiently wide to enable the pad to be inserted easily. Trim and press seams. Turn to right side and insert pad. Turn in the seam allowance on the open edges and slipstitch together.

Cushion

First motif

Commence with 10 ch, join with a ss to form a ring.

1st row Work 24 dc into ring, 1 ss into first dc.

2nd row 1 dc into same place as ss, (9 ch, miss 5 dc, 1 dc into next dc) 3 times, 9 ch, 1 ss into first dc.

3rd row Into each loop work 1 dc 1 hlf tr 12 tr 1 hlf tr and 1 dc, 1 ss into first dc.

4th row 1 ss into next hlf tr, 1 dc into same place as last ss, ★ (5 ch, miss 2 tr, 1 dc into next tr) 4 times, 5 ch, 1 dc into first half tr in next loop; repeat from ★ omitting 5 ch and 1 dc at end of last repeat, 2 ch, 1 tr into first dc.

5th row ★ 5 ch, 1 dc into next loop; repeat from ★ ending with 2 ch, 1 tr into tr of previous row.

6th row ★ 9 ch, 1 dc into next loop, (5 ch, 1 dc into next loop) 4 times; repeat from ★ omitting 5 ch and 1 dc at end of last repeat, 2 ch, 1 tr into tr of previous row.

7th row 1 dc into loop just formed, ★ into next 9 ch loop work 1 dc 1 hlf tr 6 tr 5 ch 1 ss into top of last tr (picot made) 6 tr 1 hlf tr and 1 dc, 1 dc into next loop, (5 ch, 1 dc into next loop) 3 times; repeat from ★ omitting 1 dc at end of last repeat, 1 ss into first dc. Fasten off.

Second motif

Work as first motif for 6 rows.

7th row 1 dc into loop just formed, into next 9 ch loop work 1 dc 1 hlf tr and 6 tr, 2 ch, 1 ss into any picot on first motif, 2 ch, 1 ss into last tr worked on second motif, into same loop on second motif work 6 tr 1 hlf tr and 1 dc, 1 dc into next loop (2 ch, 1 dc into next loop on first motif, 2 ch, 1 dc into next loop on second motif) 3 times, into next 9 ch loop work 1 dc 1 hlf tr and 6 tr, 2 ch, 1 ss into next picot on first motif, 2 ch, 1 ss into last tr worked on second motif, into same loop on second motif work 6 tr 1 hlf tr and 1 dc and complete as for first motif.

Make 6 rows of 7 motifs joining adjacent sides as second motif was joined to first motif.

Damp and pin out to measurements.

Coats ⚙ Mercer-Crochet No. 20 (20 grm).

3 balls. This model is worked in shade 442 (Mid Buttercup) but any other shade of Mercer-Crochet may be used.

Milward steel crochet hook 1·25 (No. 3).

1 cushion pad 14 in. × 17 in. in contrasting colour.

Size of motif 2¼ in. square
Measurements Crochet—13½ in. × 15¾ in.
Finished cushion 14 in. × 17 in.

Cheval set

Coats ✿ Mercer-Crochet No. 40 (20 grm).
2 balls. This model is worked in White, but any shade of Mercer-Crochet may be used.
⅜ yd Striped Cotton, 36 in. wide.
Milward steel crochet hook 1·00 (No. 4).

The above quantity is sufficient for 1 centrepiece and 2 small mats.

Size of motif 2 in. in diameter.

Measurements
Centrepiece 16 in.× 12 in.
Small mat 6 in. square.

Cut three pieces of striped cotton, one for centrepiece 12¾ in.× 8¾ in. and two for small mats each 2¾ in. square. Lay a small hem all round edge of each mat and sew in position.

Centrepiece

First motif

Commence with 4 ch, join with a ss to form a ring.

1st row 3 ch, 15 tr into ring, 1 ss into 3rd of 3 ch.

2nd row 1 dc into same place as last ss, ★ 3 ch, 1 dc into next tr; repeat from ★ ending with 1 ch, 1 tr into first dc.

3rd row 5 ch, 1 trip tr into loop just made, ★ 3 ch, 2 trip tr into next loop; repeat from ★ ending with 3 ch, 1 ss into 5th of 5 ch.

4th row 1 ss into next trip tr, ★ 3 dc into next sp, 7 dbl tr into 2nd of next 3 ch; repeat from ★ ending with 1 ss into first dc. Fasten off.

Second motif

Work same as first motif for 3 rows.

4th row 1 ss into next trip tr, 3 dc into next sp, 3 dbl tr into 2nd of next 3 ch,

remove hook, insert hook into 4th of 7 dbl tr of first motif and draw loop through, 4 dbl tr into same place on second motif, 3 dc into next sp, 3 dbl tr into 2nd of next 3 ch, remove hook, insert hook into 4th of 7 dbl tr of first motif and draw loop through, 4 dbl tr into same place on second motif and complete as for first motif.

Make and join 6 more motifs in same manner having 2 points free on each side between joinings.

Ninth motif

Work motif as before, joining to last motif leaving 4 points free at outside edge.

Make and join other 4 motifs leaving 2 points free between joinings.

Work other two sides to correspond, joining last motif to first motif at 2 points.

Heading

1st row Attach thread to 4th of 7 dbl tr on first free point of motif (to right of joining of any corner motif), 1 dc into same place as join, ★ 4 ch, 1 tr into 2nd of next 3 dc, 4 ch, 1 dc into 4th of next 7 dbl tr, 8 ch, 1 trip tr into 2nd of next 3 dc on same motif, 1 trip tr into 2nd of next 3 dc on next motif, 1 trip tr into 2nd of next 3 dc on next motif, 8 ch, 1 dc into 4th of next 7 dbl tr, ★ 4 ch, 1 tr into 2nd of next 3 dc, 4 ch, 1 dc into 4th of next 7 dbl tr, 8 ch, 1 trip tr into joining of motifs, 8 ch, 1 dc into 4th of next 7 dbl tr; repeat from last ★ to next corner; repeat from first ★ all round, ending with 1 ss into first dc.

2nd row 1 dc into same place as last ss, ★ 4 dc into next sp, 1 dc into next tr, 4 dc into next sp, 1 dc into next dc, 8 dc into next sp, miss 1 trip tr, 1 dc into next trip tr, miss 1 trip tr, 8 dc into next sp, 1 dc into next dc, ★ 4 dc into next sp, 1 dc into next tr, 4 dc into next sp, 1 dc into next

dc, 8 dc into next sp, 1 dc into next trip
tr, 8 dc into next sp, 1 dc into next dc;
repeat from last ★ to next corner; repeat
from first ★ all round, ending with 1 ss
into first dc. Fasten off.

Small mats (make 2)
Make 8 motifs, joining them in same
manner as centrepiece to form a square.

Heading
Work heading to correspond with centre-
piece.
Sew to edge of striped cotton.

Damp and press.

Coats ✿ Mercer–Crochet No. 40 (20 grm).
2 balls. This model is worked in shade 402 (Lt Rose Pink), but any other shade of Mercer–Crochet may be used.
Milward steel crochet hook 1·00 (No. 4).

Tension Centre Rosette $1\frac{3}{8}$ in. diameter.
Measurements
Centrepiece—$10\frac{1}{2}$ in. across
Small mat—$6\frac{1}{4}$ in. across

Cheval set

Cheval set

Centrepiece

Centre rosette

Commence with 8 ch, join with a ss to form a ring.

1st row Into ring work 16 dc, 1 ss into first dc.

2nd row 1 dc into same place as last ss, ★ 5 ch, miss 1 dc, 1 dc into next dc; repeat from ★ ending with 5 ch, 1 ss into first dc.

3rd row Into each loop work 1 dc 1 hlf tr 3 tr 1 hlf tr and 1 dc.

4th row ★ 6 ch, 1 dc into next dc of 2nd row inserting hook from back; repeat from ★ ending with 6 ch.

5th row Into each loop work 1 dc 1 hlf tr 5 tr 1 hlf tr and 1 dc.

6th row ★ 7 ch, 1 dc into next dc of 4th row inserting hook from back; repeat from ★ ending with 7 ch.

7th row Into each loop work 1 dc 1 hlf tr 5 tr 1 hlf tr and 1 dc, 1 ss into first dc. Fasten off.

First leaf

Commence with 10 ch.

1st row 1 dc into 2nd ch from hook, 1 dc into each of next 7 ch, 3 dc into next ch, 1 dc into other half of each ch, 1 ch, turn.

2nd row Miss first dc, 1 dc into each of next 8 dc working into back loop only, 3 dc into back loop of next dc, 1 dc into back loop of each of next 8 dc, 1 ch, turn.
Repeat 2nd row 8 times more.

11th row Miss first dc, 1 dc into back loop of each of next 9 dc, remove hook, insert hook into centre tr of scallop on

centre rosette and draw dropped loop through, 1 dc into same place as last dc on leaf, 1 dc into back loop of each of next 8 dc. Fasten off.

Second leaf

Work same as first leaf for 10 rows.

11th row Miss first dc, 1 dc into back loop of each of next 9 dc, remove hook, insert hook into centre tr of next scallop on centre motif and draw dropped loop through, 1 dc into same place as last dc on leaf, 1 dc into back loop of each of next 8 dc, 1 ss into turning ch of previous leaf. Fasten off.
Make and join 6 more leaves in same manner, joining last leaf to first leaf at corresponding point.

Small rosettes

Commence with 6 ch, join with a ss to form a ring.

1st row Into ring work 12 dc, 1 ss into first dc.

2nd to 4th row As 2nd to 4th row of centre rosette.

5th row Into next loop work 1 dc 1 hlf tr 2 tr, remove hook, insert hook into turning ch of 3rd row of leaf and draw dropped loop through, 3 tr 1 hlf tr and 1 dc into same loop on small rosette, into next loop work 1 dc 1 hlf tr 5 tr 1 hlf tr and 1 dc, into next loop work 1 dc 1 hlf tr 2 tr, remove hook, insert hook into corresponding side of next leaf and draw dropped loop through, 3 tr 1 hlf tr and 1 dc into same loop on small rosette, into each of next 3 loops work 1 dc 1 hlf tr 5 tr 1 hlf tr and 1 dc, 1 ss into first dc. (6 petals). Fasten off. (See illustration for position of motifs.) Make and join 7 more small rosettes between 2 leaves in same manner.

2nd group Make 8 rosettes joining first and 3rd petal of each to corresponding first free petals from the joinings between 2 rosettes on first group.

3rd group Make 8 rosettes joining first petal of each to free petal on first group.

4th group Make 8 rosettes joining first petal of each to centre free petal on second group.

5th group Two rosettes are now joined to 3rd and 4th groups thus: make a rosette, joining first petal to first free petal on 4th group rosette, now miss first free petal on next 3rd group rosette and join next petal to next petal on 3rd group rosette. Complete rosette. Make another rosette, joining first petal to centre free petal on same rosette of 3rd group, join next petal to first free petal on next 4th group rosette. Complete rosette.
Make and join 14 more rosettes in same manner.

6th group Make 8 rosettes and join between 2 rosettes of previous groups having one free petal between joinings on each rosette.

Small mat (make 2)

Work as for centrepiece until 2nd group of motifs has been completed.

Damp and press.

Edging for sheet and pillowcase

Coats ✿ Mercer-Crochet No. 20 (20 grm).
1 ball. This model is worked in shade 402 (Lt Rose Pink), but any other shade of Mercer-Crochet may be used.
1 single size sheet and Pillowcase.
Milward steel crochet hook 1·25 (No. 3).

Tension Depth of edging = $1\frac{1}{4}$ in.

Heading

Commence with 4 ch.

1st row Into 4th ch from hook work 2 tr 4 ch and 3 tr, ★ 5 ch, turn, into 4 ch sp work 3 tr 4 ch and 3 tr; repeat from ★ for length required having a multiple of 2 loops plus 1 on one side and a multiple of 2 loops on other side, ending with 9 ch.
2nd row Now work along side of first row, ★ 1 dc into next 5 ch loop, 7 ch; repeat from ★ ending with 1 hlf tr into 4th of commencing ch. Fasten off.

Edging

1st row Attach thread to first loop worked on opposite side of first row of heading, 1 dc into same loop, ★ 7 ch, 1 dc into next loop; repeat from ★ ending with 3 ch, 1 dbl tr into 4 ch loop at end of heading, 9 ch, turn.

2nd row 1 dbl tr into loop just formed, ★ into next loop work 3 tr 3 ch and 3 tr, into next loop work 1 dbl tr 5 ch and 1 dbl tr; repeat from ★ working last 1 dbl tr 5 ch and 1 dbl tr into loop after first dc, 1 ch, turn.

3rd row ★ Into next loop work (2 dc, 4 ch, 1 dc into last dc worked) twice and 1 dc, 1 dc into each of next 3 tr, 3 dc into next loop, 1 dc into each of next 3 tr; repeat from ★ omitting 9 dc at end of last repeat. Fasten off.

Damp and pin out to measurements.

Sew on edgings neatly.

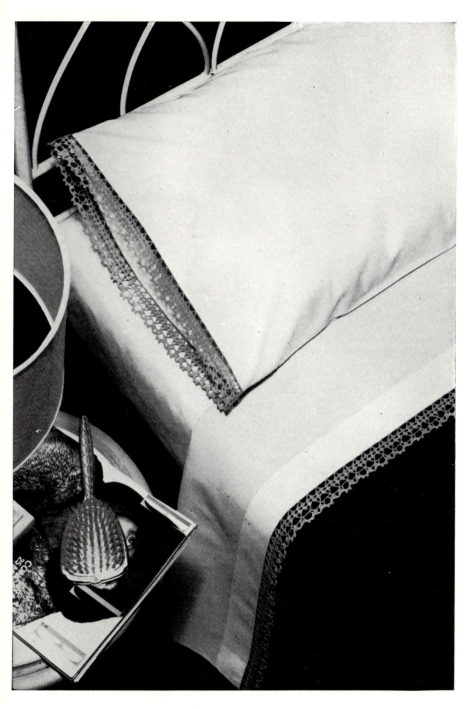

Guest towel

Coats 🟡 Mercer-Crochet No. 20 (20 grm).
1 ball. This model is worked in White, but any shade of Mercer-Crochet may be used.
Milward steel crochet hook 1·25 (No. 3).
1 guest towel.

Size of motif 2 in. in diameter.

First motif

Commence with 6 ch, join with a ss to form a ring.

1st row Into ring work 12 dc, 1 ss into first dc.

2nd row 11 ch, remove hook, miss last dc worked, insert hook into next dc and draw loop through, ★ 2 dc over loop just made, 3 ch, 1 ss into top of last dc (picot made), 2 dc into same loop, 8 ch, remove hook, miss 1 dc (to right), insert hook into next dc and draw loop through; repeat from ★ ending with 8 ch, remove hook, miss 1 dc (to right), insert hook into dc at base of first 11 ch and draw loop through, place both chains together and work 2 dc over both, 3 ch, 1 ss into top of last dc, 2 dc over chains.

3rd row ★ 3 dc into next loop, 3 ch, 1 ss into top of last dc (picot made), 3 dc into same loop, 1 dc into top dc of bar; repeat from ★ ending with 1 ss into first dc.

4th row 1 ss into next dc, 11 ch, remove hook, insert hook into 2nd of last 3 dc group and draw loop through, ★ 2 dc picot and 2 dc into loop just made, 8 ch, remove hook, insert hook into 2nd of next 3 dc group and draw loop through; repeat from ★ ending with 8 ch, remove hook, insert hook into dc at base of first 11 ch and draw loop through, place both chains together and work 2 dc over both, picot, 2 dc over both chains.

5th row ★ Into next loop work 1 hlf tr

5 tr and 1 hlf tr, 1 dc into top dc of bar; repeat from ★ ending with 1 ss into first hlf tr. Fasten off.

Second motif

Work same as first motif for 4 rows.

5th row Into next loop work 1 hlf tr 2 tr, remove hook, insert hook into 3rd of 5 tr on one point of first motif, and draw loop through, 3 tr and 1 hlf tr into same loop on second motif, 1 dc into top dc of bar, into next loop work 1 hlf tr 2 tr, remove hook, insert hook into 3rd of 5 tr of next point of first motif and draw loop through, 3 tr and 1 hlf tr into same loop on second motif, 1 dc into top dc of bar and complete as for first motif.

Make 5 more motifs joining each as second was joined to first.

Heading

Attach thread to centre tr of 6th scallop from joining of first two motifs, 1 dc into same place as join, 5 ch, 1 dc into centre tr of next scallop, 5 ch, 1 tr into first tr of next scallop, 5 ch, miss 1 tr, 1 dbl tr into next tr, 5 ch, miss 1 tr, 1 tr into next tr, ★ (5 ch, 1 dc into centre tr of next scallop) twice, 5 ch, 1 tr into first tr of next scallop, 5 ch, miss 1 tr, leaving the last loop of each on hook work 1 trip tr into next tr, 1 trip tr into centre tr of first free scallop on next motif, thread over and draw through all loops on hook, 5 ch, miss 1 tr, 1 tr into next tr; repeat from ★ ending with (5 ch, 1 dc into centre tr of next scallop) twice, 5 ch, 1 tr into first tr of next scallop, 5 ch, miss 1 tr, 1 dbl tr into next tr, 5 ch, miss 1 tr, 1 tr into next tr, (5 ch, 1 dc into centre tr of next scallop) twice. Fasten off.

Damp and pin out to measurements.

Sew edging to one end of guest towel.

Damp and press.

Corporal

Used on the altar during Mass.

Coats ✿ Mercer-Crochet No. 60 (20 grm). 4 balls White.
1 skein Clark's ⚓ Anchor Stranded Cotton, White.
1 yd linen, 36 in. wide.
Milward Steel Crochet Hook 0·75 (No. 5).

Tension 7 sps and 7 rows = 1 in.
Measurements
Corporal: 27 in. square.
Pall: 8 in. square.
Purificator: 12 in. × 28 in.

Commence with 66 ch.

1st row 1 tr into 4th ch from hook, 1 tr into each of next 2 ch (1 blk made), 2 ch, miss 2 ch, 1 tr into next ch (1 sp made), 2 more sps, 1 tr into each of next 18 ch (6 blks), 2 sps, 6 blks, 2 sps, 1 blk, 3 ch, turn.

2nd row Miss first tr, 1 tr into each of next tr (blk made over blk), 2 ch, 1 tr into next tr (sp made over sp), 1 sp, 2 ch, miss 2 tr, 1 tr into next tr (sp made over blk), 1 tr into each of next 6 tr (2 blks made over 2 blks), 2 sps, 1 blk, 2 tr into next sp, 1 tr into next tr (blk made over sp), 2 blks, 2 sps, 2 blks, 4 sps, 1 blk, 3 ch, turn.

3rd row 1 blk, 5 sps, 1 blk, 3 sps, 2 blks, 3 sps, 1 blk, 3 sps, 1 blk, turn.

4th row 1 ss into each of first 4 tr, 3 ch, 1 blk, 6 sps, 2 blks, 9 sps, 1 blk, 3 ch, turn.

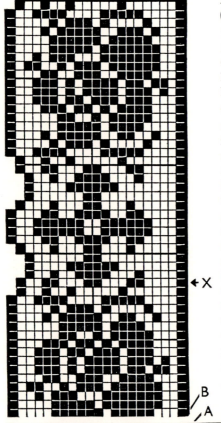

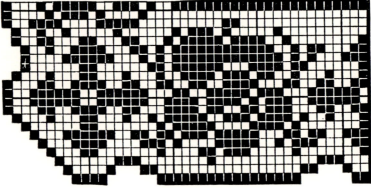

5th row 1 blk, 7 sps, 6 blks, 4 sps, 1 blk, 3 ch, turn.

6th row 1 blk, 2 sps, 1 blk, 2 sps, 4 blks, 3 sps, 1 blk, 4 sps, 1 blk, 3 ch, turn.

7th row 1 blk, 4 sps, 2 blks, 3 sps, 2 blks, 3 sps, 2 blks, 1 sp, 2 ch, miss 2 tr, make a foundation tr into 3rd st of turning ch— to make a foundation tr, thread over, insert hook into st, thread over and draw loop through, thread over and draw through 1 loop, thus making a ch st, thread over and complete as for a tr, make 3 more foundation tr by inserting hook in ch of previous foundation tr (1 blk increased), 3 ch, turn.

Follow diagram from 8th row until 41 rows are completed, turn.

42nd row 1 ss into each of first 4 tr, 3 ch, 2 tr into next sp, 1 tr into next tr, 4 sps, 1 blk, turn.

43rd row 1 ss into each of first 4 tr, 3 ch, 4 blks. Fasten off. Miss 3 blks and attach thread to last tr of same 3 blks, 3 ch, 2 blks, 3 sps, 3 ch, turn, 3 blks. Fasten off. (This completes corner.)

44th row Attach thread at 'A' on diagram, 3 ch, 1 blk, 3 sps, 5 blks, 1 sp, 6 blks, 4 sps, 1 blk, 3 ch, turn.

Follow diagram from 45th row to top. Repeat from 'X' to top of diagram, 3 times more. Make another corner as before. Continue in this manner until 4 sides are completed. Fasten off. Sew 2 short sides together.

Cut linen 22 in. square. Withdraw a thread $\frac{1}{4}$ in. from each edge and lay a small hem; dc closely over hem and into withdrawn thread. Overcast edging to dc edge.

Pall

Cut two 7 in. squares of linen and embroider a Cross at centre of one piece. Machine stitch the two pieces together across three sides, having the Cross on top. Cut a piece of cardboard $6\frac{1}{2}$ in. square, insert it between linen and sew edges of linen together.

Edging

Starting at one end, commence with 11 ch, turn.

1st row 1 tr into 8th ch from hook, 1 tr into each of next 3 ch, 5 ch, turn.

2nd row 1 tr into 4th ch from hook, 1 tr into next ch, 1 tr into each of next 4 tr, 1 tr into each of next 3 ch, 5 ch, turn.

3rd row Miss first 3 tr, 1 tr into each of next 4 tr, 5 ch, turn.

4th row Miss first 3 tr, 1 tr into next tr, 2 ch, 1 tr into 3rd of 5 turning ch, 5 ch, turn.

5th row Miss first tr, 1 tr into next tr, 1 tr into each of next 3 ch, 5 ch, turn.

The last 4 rows (2nd to 5th row inclusive) constitute the pattern. Repeat pattern until piece is long enough to go all round pall, allowing extra fullness for corners, and ending on a 4th pattern row. Fasten off. Sew two short edges together.

Edging

Join thread into sp at scallop edge, 1 dc into same sp, * 5 ch, 1 dc into turning ch at end of Cross, 5 ch, 1 dc into next sp; repeat from * all round ending with 1 ss into first dc.

On next row make 7 dc into first loop, * 5 ch, 7 dc into each of next two 5 ch loops; repeat from * all round omitting 7 dc at end of last repeat, 1 ss into first dc. Fasten off. Sew all round edges of pall.

Purificator

Cut a piece of linen 13 in. × $24\frac{1}{2}$ in. Make a 1 in. hem along both short sides and a $\frac{1}{4}$ in. hem along other two sides. Embroider a Cross in centre of linen.

Edging

Starting at 'B' on diagrams, commence with 66 ch, and follow diagram to top, then repeat design from 'X' to top until piece measures 12 in. Fasten off.
Make another piece the same and sew edging to each end of linen.

Coats ⚙ Mercer-Crochet No. 20 (20
grm). 2 balls. This model is worked in
shade 610 (Dark Ecru), but any other
shade of Mercer-Crochet may be used.
Milward steel crochet hook 1·25
(No. 3).

Gloves

Gloves

Tension 5 sps and 5 rows = 1 in. on palm.
Size of Glove 6½ in.

LEFT HAND

Palm

Little finger

Commence with 115 ch.

1st row 1 tr into 7th ch from hook, * 2 ch, miss 2 ch, 1 tr into next ch; repeat from * 35 times more (37 sps), 5 ch, turn.

2nd row 1 tr into first sp, * 2 ch, 1 tr into next sp; repeat from * to second last sp, into last sp work (2 ch, 1 tr) twice, 5 ch, turn.

3rd row 1 tr into first sp, * 2 ch, 1 tr into next sp; repeat from * 35 times more, 2 ch, 1 tr into 3rd of 5 ch, 5 ch, turn.

4th row 1 tr into first sp, * 2 ch, 1 tr into next sp; repeat from * 35 times more, 1 tr into 3rd of 5 ch, 5 ch, turn.

5th row 1 tr into first 2 ch sp, * 2 ch, 1 tr into next sp; repeat from * 7 times more, 2 ch, 1 hlf tr into next sp, 2 ch, 1 dc into next sp, 48 ch.

Ring finger

1st row 1 tr into 7th ch from hook, * 2 ch, miss 2 ch, 1 tr into next ch; repeat from * 12 times more, 2 ch, 1 tr into same place as dc of previous finger, ** 2 ch, 1 tr into next sp on palm; repeat from ** 24 times more, 2 ch, 1 tr into 3rd of 5 ch, 5 ch, turn.

2nd row 1 tr into first sp, * 2 ch, 1 tr into next sp; repeat from * to second last sp, into last sp work (2 ch, 1 tr) twice, 5 ch, turn.

3rd row 1 tr into first sp, * 2 ch, 1 tr into next sp; repeat from * to second last sp, 2 ch, 1 tr into 3rd of 5 ch, 5 ch, turn.

4th row As 3rd row, ending with 1 tr into 3rd of 5 ch, 5 ch, turn.

5th row 1 tr into first 2 ch sp, * 2 ch, 1 tr into next sp; repeat from * 10 times more, 2 ch, 1 hlf tr into next sp, 2 ch, 1 dc into next sp, 51 ch.

Middle finger

1st row 1 tr into 7th ch from hook, * 2 ch, miss 2 ch, 1 tr into next ch; repeat from * 13 times more, 2 ch, 1 tr into same place as dc of previous finger, ** 2 ch, 1 tr into next sp on palm; repeat from ** 25 times more, 2 ch, 1 tr into 3rd of 5 ch, 5 ch, turn.

2nd to 4th row As 2nd to 4th row of Ring Finger.

5th row 1 tr into first 2 ch sp, * 2 ch, 1 tr into next sp; repeat from * 12 times more, 2 ch, 1 hlf tr into next sp, 2 ch, 1 dc into next sp, 45 ch.

Fore finger

1st row 1 tr into 7th ch from hook, * 2 ch, miss 2 ch, 1 tr into next ch; repeat from * 11 times more, 2 ch, 1 tr into same place as dc of previous finger, ** 2 ch, 1 tr into next sp on palm; repeat from ** 25 times more, 2 ch, 1 tr into 3rd of 5 ch, 5 ch, turn.

2nd to 4th row As 2nd to 4th row of Ring Finger.

5th row 1 tr into first 2 ch sp, * 2 ch, 1 tr into next sp; repeat from * 17 times more, 2 ch, 1 hlf tr into next sp, 2 ch, 1 dc into next sp 40 ch.

Thumb

1st row 1 tr into 7th ch from hook, * 2 ch, miss 2 ch, 1 tr into next ch; repeat from * 10 times more, 2 ch, 1 tr into same place as dc of palm, (2 ch, 1 tr into next sp) twice, 2 ch, 1 hlf tr into next sp, 2 ch, 1 dc into next sp, 3 ch, turn.

2nd row Miss first sp, 1 dc into next sp, 2 ch, 1 hlf tr into next sp, * 2 ch, 1 tr into next sp; repeat from * to second last sp, into last sp work (2 ch, 1 tr) twice, 5 ch, turn.

3rd row 1 tr into first sp, * 2 ch, 1 tr into next sp; repeat from * 15 times more, 2 ch, 1 tr into same place as last dc of first row, (2 ch, 1 tr into next sp) twice, 2 ch, 1 hlf tr into next sp, 2 ch, 1 dc into next sp, 3 ch, turn.

4th row As 2nd row ending with 1 tr into 3rd of 5 ch, 5 ch, turn.

5th row 1 tr into first 2 ch sp, * 2 ch, 1 tr into next sp; repeat from * 18 times more, 2 ch, 1 tr into same place as last dc of 3rd row, (2 ch, 1 tr into next sp) twice, 2 ch, 1 hlf tr into next sp, 2 ch, 1 dc into next sp, 3 ch, turn.

6th row As 2nd row ending with 1 tr into 3rd of 5 turning ch. Fasten off.

BACK OF HAND

Commence at wrist with 64 ch.

84

1st row 1 tr into 10th ch from hook, 1 tr into each of next 2 ch, ★ 3 ch, miss 3 ch, 1 tr into each of next 3 ch; repeat from ★ 7 times more, 3 ch, miss 3 ch, 1 tr into last ch, 3 ch, turn.

2nd row Into first sp work 2 tr 1 ch and 2 tr, ★ into next sp work 2 tr 1 ch and 2 tr; repeat from ★ 8 times more, 1 tr into 6th of turning ch, 6 ch, turn.

3rd row 2 tr into first 1 ch sp, ★ 3 ch, 2 tr into next 1 ch sp; repeat from ★ 8 times more, 3 ch, 1 tr into 3rd of 3 ch, 3 ch, turn.

4th row 2 tr into first sp, ★ into next sp work 2 tr 1 ch and 2 tr; repeat from ★ 8 times more, 2 tr into last sp, 1 tr into 3rd of 6 ch, 3 ch, turn.

5th row 1 tr into first tr, ★ 3 ch, 2 tr into next 1 ch sp; repeat from ★ 8 times more, 3 ch, 1 tr into last tr, 1 tr into 3rd of 3 ch, 3 ch, turn.

6th row As 2nd row ending with 1 tr into 3rd of 3 ch, 6 ch, turn.
Repeat 3rd to 6th row 5 times more.

Little finger

1st row 2 tr into first 1 ch sp, 3 ch, 2 tr into next 1 ch sp, 3 ch, miss 1 tr, 1 tr into next tr, 3 ch, turn.

2nd row 2 tr into first sp, into next sp work 2 tr 1 ch and 2 tr, 2 tr into last sp, 1 tr into 3rd of 6 ch, 3 ch, turn.
Continue to work in pattern for 8 more rows.

11th row 1 tr into first tr, 1 ch, 2 tr into next 1 ch sp, 1 ch, 1 tr into last tr, 1 tr into 3rd of 3 ch. Fasten off.

Ring finger

1st row Join thread into same place as last tr on first row of previous finger, 6 ch, (2 tr into next 1 ch sp, 3 ch) 3 times, miss 1 tr, 1 tr into next tr, 3 ch, turn.

2nd row 2 tr into first sp, (into next sp work 2 tr 1 ch and 2 tr) twice, 2 tr into last sp, 1 tr into 3rd of 6 ch, 3 ch, turn.
Continue to work in pattern for 12 more rows.

15th row 1 tr into first tr, 1 ch, (2 tr into next 1 ch sp, 1 ch) twice, 1 tr into last tr, 1 tr into 3rd of 3 turning ch. Fasten off.

Middle finger

1st row Join thread into top of last tr on first row of previous finger, 3 ch, (2 tr into next 1 ch sp, 3 ch) 3 times, miss 1 tr, 1 tr into next tr, 3 ch, turn.

2nd row 2 tr into first sp, (into next sp work 2 tr 1 ch and 2 tr) twice, 2 tr into next sp, 1 tr into same place as join, 3 ch, turn.
Continue to work in pattern for 14 more rows, turning with 4 ch on last row.

17th row (2 tr into next 1 ch sp, 1 ch) 3 times, 1 tr into 3rd of 3 turning ch. Fasten off.

Fore finger

1st row Join thread into top of last tr on first row of previous finger, 3 ch, (2 tr into next 1 ch sp, 3 ch) twice, 1 tr into 3rd of 3 ch, 3 ch, turn.

2nd row 2 tr into first sp, into next sp work 2 tr 1 ch and 2 tr, 2 tr into last sp, 1 tr into same place as join, 3 ch, turn.
Continue to work in pattern for 12 more rows.

15th row 1 tr into first tr, 1 ch, 2 tr into next 1 ch sp, 1 ch, 1 tr into last tr, 1 tr into 3rd of 3 ch. Fasten off.
Join thread to base of last tr worked on first row of back of hand, 5 ch, 1 tr over first row-end, ★ 2 ch, 1 tr over next row-end; repeat from ★ to within 2 rows from top of fore finger, 2 ch, 1 hlf tr over next row-end, 2 ch, 1 dc over last row-end, 3 ch, turn.

Next row 1 dc into first 2 ch sp, 2 ch, 1 hlf tr into next sp, ★ 2 ch, 1 tr into next sp; repeat from ★ 16 times more, 2 ch, 1 hlf tr into next sp, 2 ch, 1 dc into next sp, 40 ch.

Thumb

1st row 1 tr into 7th ch from hook, ★ 2 ch, miss 2 ch, 1 tr into next ch; repeat from ★ 10 times more, 2 ch, 1 tr into same place as last dc on back of hand, (2 ch, 1 tr into next sp) twice, 2 ch, 1 hlf tr into next tr, 2 ch, 1 dc into next sp, 3 ch, turn.

2nd row As 2nd row of front of thumb.

3rd row 1 tr into first sp, ★ 2 ch, 1 tr into next sp; repeat from ★ 15 times more, 2 ch, 1 tr into same place as last dc of first row, (2 ch, 1 tr into next sp) twice, 2 ch, 1 hlf tr into next sp, 2 ch, 1 dc into next sp, 3 ch, turn.

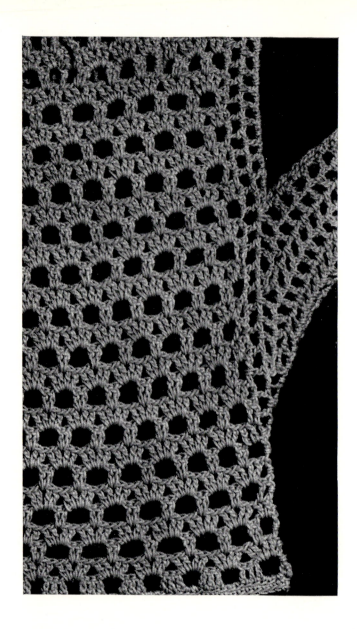

4th row As 4th row of front of thumb.

5th row 1 tr into first 2 ch sp, ★ 2 ch, 1 tr into next sp; repeat from ★ 18 times more, 2 ch, 1 tr into same place as last dc of 3rd row, (2 ch, 1 tr into next sp) twice, 2 ch, 1 hlf tr into next tr, 2 ch, 1 dc into next sp, 3 ch, turn.

6th row As 6th row of front of thumb. Fasten off.

Place back and front of glove together and join as follows:

Join thread into first sp at side of back of hand, 1 dc into same place as join, 1 ch,

1 dc into first sp on palm, (1 ch, 1 dc into next sp on back, 1 ch, 1 dc into next sp on palm) 6 times, 1 ch, 1 dc into first sp on back thumb, 1 ch, 1 dc into first sp on front thumb, (* 1 ch, 1 dc into next sp on back thumb, 1 ch, 1 dc into next sp on front thumb *) 22 times, (1 ch, 1 dc into next row-end on back thumb, 1 ch, 1 dc into next row-end on front thumb) 6 times, repeat from * to * 12 times, 1 ch, 1 dc into first sp on back fore finger, 1 ch, 1 dc into first sp on front fore finger, (1 ch, 1 dc into next sp on back fore finger, 1 ch, 1 dc into next sp on front fore finger) 20 times, (1 ch, 1 dc into next tr at back finger tip, 1 ch, 1 dc into next row-end on front finger tip, 1 ch, 1 dc into next sp on back finger, 1 ch, 1 dc into next row-end on front finger) 3 times, continue to join fingers in this manner.

Wrist

1st row Attach yarn into any seam and work a row of dc all round wrist working 3 dc into each sp and 1 dc between tr on first row of back of hand and 3 dc over each row-end at front, 1 ss into first dc.

2nd row 1 dc into same place as ss, 1 dc into each dc, 1 ss into first dc. Fasten off.
If a deeper wrist is desired work more rows of dc.

RIGHT HAND

Palm

Work same as Left Hand and reverse when joining.

Back of hand

Work same as Left Hand for 26 rows.
Now work fingers from fore finger to little finger as follows:

Fore finger

1st row As first row of Little Finger on left hand.

2nd row 2 tr into first sp, into next sp work 2 tr 1 ch and 2 tr, 2 tr into last sp, 1 tr into 3rd of 6 ch, 3 ch, turn,
Continue to work in pattern for 12 more rows.

15th row As 15th row of Fore Finger on left hand.

Middle finger

1st row Join thread into top of first tr on first row of previous finger and complete as 1st row of Middle Finger on left hand.

2nd to 17th row As 2nd to 17th row of Middle Finger on left hand.

Ring finger

1st and 2nd rows As 1st and 2nd rows of Middle Finger on left hand.
Continue in pattern for 12 more rows.

15th row As 15th row of Ring Finger on left hand.

Little finger

1st row Join thread into same place as last tr on first row of Ring Finger, 6 ch, (2 tr into next 1 ch sp, 3 ch) twice, 1 tr into 3rd of 3 ch, 3 ch, turn.

2nd to 11th row As 2nd to 11th row of Little Finger on left hand.
With wrong side facing join thread over turning ch on first row of back of hand, 5 ch, 1 tr over same row-end, * 2 ch, 1 tr over next row-end; repeat from * to within 2 rows from top of fore finger, 2 ch, 1 hlf tr over next row-end, 2 ch, 1 dc over last row-end, 3 ch, turn.

Next row 1 dc into first 2 ch sp, 2 ch, 1 hlf tr into next sp, * 2 ch, 1 tr into next sp; repeat from * 16 times more, 2 ch, 1 hlf tr into next sp, 2 ch, 1 dc into next sp, 40 ch.

Thumb

Work same as back half of thumb.
Place back and front of glove together and join to correspond with Left Hand.
Work wrist as for Left Hand.

Damp and press.

Motif stole

Coats ✿ Mercer-Crochet No. 20 (20 grm).
25 balls. **This model is worked in Black, but any shade of Mercer-Crochet may be used.**
Milward steel crochet hook 1·25 (No. 3).

Size of motif 1¾ in. in diameter.
Measurements 24½ in. × 73½ in.

First motif

Commence with 6 ch.

1st row Into 6th ch from hook work (1 tr, 2 ch) 7 times, 1 ss into 4th of 6 ch.

2nd row 1 ss into first sp, 1 dc into same sp, ★ (5 ch, 1 ss into 4th ch from hook—picot made) twice, 1 ch, 1 dc into next sp; repeat from ★ omitting 1 dc at end of last repeat, 1 ss into first dc.

3rd row Ss along to ch between next 2 picots on next loop, 1 dc into same loop, ★ 7 ch, 1 dc between picots of next loop; repeat from ★ omitting 1 dc at end of last repeat, 1 ss into first dc.

4th row Into each loop work (1 dc 1 hlf tr 9 tr 1 hlf tr and 1 dc) 1 ss into first dc. (8 scallops). Fasten off.

Second motif

Work as first motif for 3 rows.

4th row Into first loop work 1 dc 1 hlf tr 4 tr, 1 ss into centre tr of any scallop of first motif, 5 tr 1 hlf tr and 1 dc into same loop on second motif, into next loop work 1 dc 1 hlf tr 4 tr, 1 ss into centre tr of next scallop on first motif, 5 tr 1 hlf tr and 1 dc into same loop on second motif, complete as for first motif.

Make 14 rows of 42 motifs, joining each as second motif was joined to first motif.

Filling

Commence with 7 ch, join with a ss to form a ring.

1st row 1 dc into ring, 4 ch, 1 ss into any join between motifs, 4 ch, (1 dc into ring, 4 ch, 1 ss into next joining between motifs, 4 ch) 3 times, 1 ss into first dc. Fasten off.
Fill in all spaces between motifs in same manner.

Damp and pin out to measurements.

Collar

Coats ⚙ Mercer–Crochet No. 40 (20 grm).

1 ball. This model is worked in shade 510 (Cobalt Blue), but any other shade of Mercer-Crochet may be used. Collar.

Milward steel crochet hook 1·00 (No. 4).

Size of motif. 1 in. in diameter.

First motif

Commence with 6 ch.

1st row 1 dbl tr into 6th ch from hook, * 2 ch, 1 dbl tr into same ch as last dbl tr; repeat from * 9 times more, 2 ch, 1 ss into 4th of 6 ch. (12 sps).

2nd row 3 dc into each 2 ch sp.

3rd row 1 dc into first dc, * 1 dc 4 ch and 1 dc into next dc, 1 dc into each of next 2 dc; repeat from * omitting 1 dc at end of last repeat, 1 ss into first dc. Fasten off.

Second motif

Work same as first motif for 2 rows.

3rd row 1 dc into first dc, 1 dc into next dc, 2 ch, 1 ss into corresponding picot of first motif, 2 ch, 1 dc into same dc of second motif, 1 dc into each of next 3 dc, 2 ch, 1 ss into next picot of first motif, 2 ch, 1 dc into same dc of second motif and complete as for first motif.

Make and join sufficient motifs to go round edge of collar, joining each motif as second was joined to first, leaving 4 picots free on each side of joining.

Heading

Attach thread to 4th free picot (from joining between motifs) on end motif, 8 ch, * 1 dc into next picot, 3 ch, 1 dc into next picot, 4 ch, leaving the last loop of each on hook work 1 dbl tr into each of next 2 free picots, thread over and

draw through all loops on hook (a joint dbl tr made), 4 ch; repeat from * ending with 1 dc into next picot, 3 ch, 1 dc into next picot, 4 ch, 1 dbl tr into next picot. Fasten off.

Sew round edge of collar.

Damp and press.

Collar and cuffs

Tension First 4 rows and 6 sps= 1 in.
Measurements

Depth of each collar $2\frac{3}{4}$ in.
Depth of each cuff $1\frac{3}{4}$ in.
To fit neckband $14\frac{1}{2}$ ($17\frac{1}{2}$) in.
To fit edge of sleeve $8\frac{1}{2}$ (10) in.

Instructions for larger neckband are given in brackets

Collar

Commence with 174 (210) ch, to measure approx $14\frac{1}{2}$ ($17\frac{1}{2}$) in.

1st row 1 tr into 6th ch from hook, ★ 1 ch, miss 1 ch, 1 tr into next ch; repeat from ★ ending with 5 ch, turn. 85 (103) sps.

2nd row (right side): 1 trip tr into first sp, miss 2 sps, ★ leaving the last loop of each on hook work 2 trip tr into next sp, thread over and draw through all loops on hook (a 2 trip tr cluster made), 5 ch, a 2 trip tr cluster into same sp, miss 2 sps; repeat from ★ ending with a 2 trip tr cluster into last sp, 4 ch, turn.

3rd row Miss first 2 clusters, 1 tr into next ch, ★ (1 ch, miss 1 ch, 1 tr into next ch) twice, 1 ch, 1 tr into next cluster, 1 ch, 1 tr into next ch; repeat from ★ omitting 1 ch and 1 tr at end of last repeat, 4 ch, turn. 108 (132) sps.

4th row 1 tr into first sp, ★ 1 ch, 1 tr into next sp; repeat from ★ ending with 1 ch, 1 tr into last sp, 1 ch, 1 tr into 3rd of 4 ch, 4 ch, turn. 109 (133) sps.

5th row Miss first sp, 1 tr into next sp, ★ 1 ch, 1 tr into next sp; repeat from ★ ending with 1 ch, 1 tr into last sp, 1 ch, 1 tr into 3rd of 4 ch, 5 ch, turn. 109 (133) sps.

6th row As 2nd row.

7th row As 3rd row. 140 (172) sps.

8th row As 4th (5th) row. 141 (172) sps.

9th row As 4th (5th) row, 5 ch, turn. 142 (172) sps.

10th row As 2nd row.

11th row As 3rd row. Fasten off.

Heading

1st row With wrong side facing, attach thread to first of foundation ch, 4 ch, 1 dbl tr into each of next 170 (206) ch, 4 ch, turn.

2nd row Miss first dbl tr, 1 dbl tr into each dbl tr, 1 dbl tr into 4th of 4 ch. Fasten off.

Edging

With right side facing and working along short side, attach thread to last sp on first row, 2 dc into same sp, (5 dc over next row-end, 2 dc into each of next 3 row-ends) twice, 5 dc over next row-end, 4 dc into next sp, ★ 1 dc into next tr, 1 dc into next sp; repeat from ★ along edge of collar, then complete other side to correspond.

Coats ❁ Mercer-Crochet No. 20 (20 grm).
2 balls. Shade 510 (Cobalt Blue), but any other shade of Mercer-Crochet may be used.
Milward steel crochet hook 1·25 (No. 3).

Cuff (make 2)

Commence with 102 (120) ch, to measure approx 8½ (10) in. and work as collar for 4 rows, 5 ch, turn.

5th row As 2nd row of collar.

6th row As 3rd row of collar. Fasten off.

Heading

1st row Attach thread to first of foundation ch, 4 ch, 1 dbl tr into each of next 98 (116) ch, 4 ch, turn.

2nd row As 2nd row of heading for collar.

Edging

Attach thread to last sp on first row, 2 dc into same sp, 5 dc over next row-end, 2 dc over each of next 2 row-ends, 5 dc over next row-end, 4 dc into next sp, ★ 1 dc into next tr, 1 dc into next sp; repeat from ★ along edge of cuff then complete other side to correspond.

Damp and pin out to measurements.

Sew collar and cuffs in position on blouse.

Collar and cuffs

Collar

Commence with a length of chain to measure length of neck edge, having a multiple of 6 ch plus 2.

1st row 1 tr into 8th ch from hook, ★ 2 ch, miss 2 ch, 1 tr into next ch; repeat from ★ to end, 5 ch, turn.

2nd row Miss first tr, ★ 1 tr into next tr, 2 ch; repeat from ★ ending with 1 tr into 3rd of turning ch, 5 ch, turn.
Repeat 2nd row 6 times more, turning with 1 ch at end of last row.

Edging

1 dc into first sp, ★ 5 tr into next sp (shell made), 1 dc into next sp; repeat from ★ working last dc into corner sp, 3 dc into same sp, (3 dc into next sp) 6 times, 6 dc into next corner sp, 2 dc into each sp to within corner sp, 6 dc into corner sp, (3 dc into next sp) 6 times, 3 dc into next sp, 1 ss into first dc. Fasten off.

Shell frills

1st row With right side facing attach thread to 5th of 8 turning ch on 7th row, 1 dc into next sp, a shell into next sp, ★ 1 dc into next sp, a shell into next sp; repeat from ★ omitting a shell at end of last repeat. Fasten off. Repeat first row twice more on 6th and 5th rows.

Cuff (make 2)

Commence with a length of chain to measure length of cuff edge, having a multiple of 6 ch plus 2 and complete to correspond with collar.

Damp and pin out to measurements.

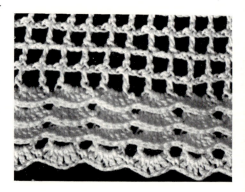

Coats ✿ Mercer-Crochet No. 20 (20 grm).
2 balls. This model is worked in White, but any shade of Mercer-Crochet may be used.
Milward steel crochet hook 1·25 (No. 3).

Tension 5 sps and 5 rows= 1 in.
Measurements Depth of collar and cuffs 1⅞ in.

Crochet tie with star stitch

Coats 🕸 Mercer-Crochet No. 20 (20 grm).
2 balls. This model is worked in 477 (Tan), but any other shade of Mercer-Crochet may be used.
Milward steel crochet hook 1·25 (No. 3).
¾ yd ribbon 1½ in. wide in contrasting colour for lining.

Tension 4 stars and 3 rows = 1½ in.
Measurements
Width of finished tie   1½ in.
Length   53 in. (adjustable).

Commence with 36 ch.

1st row 1 hlf tr into 3rd ch from hook, 1 hlf tr into each remaining ch, 3 ch, turn.

2nd row Insert hook into 2nd ch from hook and draw loop through, insert hook into next ch and draw loop through, (insert hook into back loop of next hlf tr and draw loop through) 3 times (6 loops on hook), thread over and draw through all loops on hook, 1 ch to form eye (star made), ★ insert hook into eye of last star and draw loop through, insert hook into last loop of last star and draw loop through, insert hook into st already worked into and draw loop through, (insert hook into back loop of next hlf tr and draw loop through) twice (6 loops on hook), thread over and draw through all loops on hook, 1 ch to form eye (another star made); repeat from ★ across, 1 hlf tr into last st worked into, 2 ch, turn. (17 star sts).

3rd row 1 hlf tr into first eye, 2 hlf tr into each eye across, 1 hlf tr into top of turning ch, 3 ch, turn.
Repeat 2nd and 3rd rows until work measures 17½ in. turning with 2 ch at end

of last row. Main section completed; remainder of tie is worked in hlf tr lifting back half of each st throughout on previous row.

Next row Miss first hlf tr, thread over hook, insert into next st and draw loop through, insert hook into next st and draw loop through, thread over and draw through all loops on hook (a decrease made), 1 hlf tr into each hlf tr to within last 3 sts, a decrease over next 2 sts, 1 hlf tr into top of turning ch, 2 ch, turn.
Repeat last row 8 times more. (17 sts).
Continue without shaping for 5 in.
Repeat decrease row twice. (13 sts).
Continue without shaping until work measures 30 in. (or length required) from last decrease. Fasten off.

Damp and press.

To make up

Turn back ¼ in. on raw edges of ribbon and place centrally on wrong side of main section. Turn back crochet edges on each side and slipstitch in position to ribbon.

Crochet tie with popcorn stitch

Coats 🪡 Mercer-Crochet No. 20 (20 grm).
2 balls. This model is worked in shade 513 (Orange), but any other shade of Mercer-Crochet may be used.
Milward steel crochet hook 1·25 (No. 3).
¾ yd ribbon 1½ in. wide in contrasting colour for lining.

Tension First 6 rows   1 in.
Measurements
Width of finished tie   1½ in.
Length 44 in. (adjustable).
Commence with 33 ch.

1st row (right side) 1 tr into 4th ch from hook, 1 tr into each ch, 3 ch, turn.

2nd row Miss first tr, 1 tr into each tr, 1 tr into 3rd of 3 ch, 3 ch, turn.

3rd row Miss first tr, 1 tr into each of next 3 tr, * 2 ch, miss 2 tr, 1 tr into next tr, 3 ch, miss 2 tr, 4 tr into next tr, remove loop from hook, insert hook into ch before tr group and into dropped loop and draw loop through (a popcorn stitch made); repeat from * 3 times more, omitting 1 ch and a popcorn st at end of last repeat, miss 2 tr, 1 tr into each of next 3 tr, 1 tr into 3rd of 3 ch, 1 ch, turn.

4th row 1 dc into each of first 4 tr, * 2 dc into next sp, 1 dc into next tr, 2 dc into next sp, 1 dc into next popcorn st; repeat from * 3 times more, omitting 1 dc at end of last repeat, 1 dc into each of next 3 tr, 1 dc into 3rd of 3 ch, 3 ch, turn.

5th row Miss first dc, 1 tr into each of next 3 dc, * 3 ch, miss 2 dc, 1 popcorn st into next dc, 2 ch, miss 2 dc, 1 tr into next dc; repeat from * 3 times more, 1 tr into each of next 3 dc, 1 ch, turn.

6th row 1 dc into each of first 4 tr, * 2 dc into next sp, 1 dc into next popcorn st, 2 dc into next sp, 1 dc into next tr; repeat from * 3 times more, 1 dc into each of next 2 tr, 1 dc into 3rd of 3 ch, 3 ch, turn.

7th row Miss first dc, 1 tr into each dc, 3 ch, turn.

Repeat 2nd to 7th row until work measures 18 in. or length required ending with a 7th row.

Next row Miss first tr, leaving the last loop of each on hook work 1 tr into each of next 2 tr, thread over and draw through all loops on hook (a decrease made), 1 tr into each tr to within last 3 sts, a decrease over next 2 sts, 1 tr into 3rd of 3 ch, 3 ch, turn.

Next 2 rows Miss first tr, 1 tr into each st, 3 ch, turn.
Repeat last 3 rows 8 times more. (13 sts).

Next row Miss first tr, 1 tr into each tr, 1 tr into 3rd of 3 ch, 3 ch, turn.
Repeat last row until work measures 22 in., or length required, from last decrease row, omitting turning ch at end of last row.
Fasten off.

Dampen and press.

To make up
Turn back ¼ in. on raw edges of ribbon and place centrally on wrong side of main section. Turn back crochet edges on each side and slipstitch in position to ribbon.

Edging No. 1

Coats ⚙ Mercer-Crochet No. 40 (20 grm).
1 ball. This model is worked in White but any shade of Mercer-Crochet may be used.
Milward steel crochet hook 1·00 (No. 4).
1 handkerchief.

Depth of edging ¾ in.

Edging No. 2

Coats ⚙ Mercer-Crochet No. 40 (20 grm).
1 ball. This model is worked in shade 582 (Straw Yellow), but any other shade of Mercer-Crochet may be used.

Handkerchief edgings

1 handkerchief.
Milward steel crochet hook 1·00 (No. 4).
Depth of edging ¾ in.

Edging No. 3

Coats ⚙ Mercer-Crochet No. 40 (20 grm).
1 ball. This model is worked in shade 503 (Coral Pink), but any other shade of Mercer-Crochet may be used.
1 handkerchief.
Milward steel crochet hook 1·00 (No. 4).
Depth of edging ¾ in.

99

Edging No. 1

Side

Commence with 17 ch.

1st row 1 dc into 11th ch from hook, 1 dc into each of next 2 ch, 3 ch, miss 3 ch, 1 dbl tr into next ch, 1 ch, turn.

2nd row 1 dc into first dbl tr, 4 ch, leaving the last loop of each on hook work 2 dbl tr into 4th ch from hook, thread over and draw through all loops on hook (a 2 dbl tr cluster made), miss 1 dc, 1 trip tr into next dc, 4 ch, a 2 dbl tr cluster into 4th ch from hook, miss 3 ch, 1 dc into next ch, 10 ch, turn.

3rd row A 2 dbl tr cluster into 4th ch from hook, 1 ss into next trip tr, 4 ch, a 2 dbl tr cluster into 4th ch from hook, 1 quad tr into next dc, 1 ch, turn.

4th row 1 dc into first quad tr, 4 ch, miss first cluster, 1 trip tr into same place as ss, 4 ch, miss next cluster, 1 dc into next ch, 7 ch, turn.

5th row Miss first dc and 3 ch, 1 dc into next ch, 1 dc into next trip tr, 1 dc into next ch, 3 ch, 1 dbl tr into next dc, 1 ch, turn.

Repeat 2nd to 5th row to fit one side of handkerchief.

Corner

1st row 1 dc into first dbl tr, 4 ch, a 2 dbl tr cluster into 4th ch from hook, miss 1 dc, 1 trip tr into next dc, 4 ch, turn.

2nd row A 2 dbl tr cluster into 4th ch from hook, 1 quad tr into next dc, 6 ch, turn.

3rd row A 3 dbl tr cluster into trip tr of 1st row of corner, 4 ch, 1 trip tr into same place as last cluster, 4 ch, 1 dc into 4th of 7 ch on last row of side, 7 ch, turn.

4th row Miss first dc and 3 ch, 1 dc into next ch, 1 dc into next trip tr, 1 dc into next ch, 3 ch, 1 dbl tr into next cluster, 1 ch, turn.

Repeat from 2nd row of side 3 times more omitting 4th row of corner at end of last repeat. Fasten off. Oversew top of last row neatly to foundation ch.

Heading

With right side facing, attach thread to first sp after any corner, 4 dc into same sp, ★ 8 dc into next sp, 4 dc into next sp; repeat from ★ along side, 4 dc into next sp; repeat from first ★ omitting 4 dc at end of last repeat, 1 ss into first dc.

Edging

With right side facing, attach thread to cluster at any corner, into same place as join work 1 dc 3 ch and 1 dc, ★ into next sp work 2 dc 3 ch 4 dc 3 ch and 2 dc, into next sp work 2 dc 3 ch and 2 dc; repeat from ★ along side, ending with 2 dc 3 ch 4 dc 3 ch and 2 dc into last sp, into next cluster work 1 dc 3 ch and 1 dc; repeat from first ★ omitting 1 dc 3 ch and 1 dc at end of last repeat, 1 ss into first dc. Fasten off.

Damp and pin out to measurements.

Oversew neatly to edge of handkerchief.

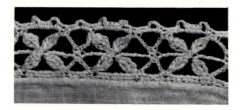

Edging No. 2

Commence with 7 ch.

1st row 1 dbl tr into 7th ch from hook, ★ 6 ch, 1 dbl tr into top of last dbl tr; repeat from ★ until there is sufficient to go all round handkerchief, ending with 1 ss into first ch worked.

2nd row 1 ss into each of next 3 ch, 7 ch, leaving the last loop of each on hook work 2 dbl tr into 4th ch from hook, thread over and draw through all loops on hook (a 2 dbl tr cluster made), ★ 1 tr into next loop, 4 ch, a 2 dbl tr cluster into 4th ch from hook; repeat from ★ along side, 1 dbl tr into next dbl tr, 4 ch, a 2 dbl tr cluster into 4th ch from hook, 1 dbl tr into same place as last dbl tr (corner turned), 4 ch, a 2 dbl tr cluster into 4th ch from hook; repeat from first ★ ending with 1 ss into base of first cluster.

3rd row 4 ch, 1 dbl tr into next tr, ★ 6 ch, 1 tr into 5th ch from hook, 1 ch, leaving the last loop of each on hook, work 1 dbl tr into same place as last dbl tr and 1 dbl tr into next tr, thread over and draw through all loops on hook (a joint dbl tr made); repeat from ★ along side, 6 ch, 1 tr into 5th ch from hook, 1 ch, 1 dbl tr into same dbl tr, 6 ch, 1 tr into 5th ch from hook, 1 ch, 1 dbl tr into next dbl tr; repeat from first ★ ending with 6 ch, 1 tr into 5th ch from hook, 1 ch, 1 ss into first dbl tr. Fasten off.

Damp and pin out to measurements.

Oversew neatly to edge of handkerchief.

2nd row 1 ss into each of next 3 ch, 1 dc into same loop, ★ 4 ch, leaving the last loop of each on hook work 3 dbl tr into next dc, thread over and draw through all loops on hook (a 3 dbl tr cluster made), 5 ch, into same place work a 3 dbl tr cluster 5 ch and a 3 dbl tr cluster, 4 ch, miss next sp, 1 dc into next loop; repeat from ★ to next corner, 4 ch, into next dc work (a 3 dbl tr cluster, 5 ch) twice and a 3 dbl tr cluster, 4 ch, 1 dc into next loop, 4 ch, into next dc work (a 3 dbl tr cluster, 5 ch) twice and a 3 dbl tr cluster, 4 ch, miss next sp, 1 dc into next loop, 4 ch; repeat from first ★ omitting 1 dc and 4 ch at end of last repeat, 1 ss into first dc.

3rd row ★ 3 dc into next loop, 3 ch, (5

Edging No. 3

Commence with 7 ch.

1st row 1 dbl tr into 7th ch from hook, ★ 10 ch, 1 dbl tr into top of last dbl tr, 1 ch, turn, 1 dc into first dbl tr, 4 ch, miss 4 ch, 1 dc into next ch, 6 ch, turn, miss 1 dc, 1 dbl tr into next dc, 6 ch, 1 dbl tr into last dbl tr; repeat from ★ until there is sufficient for one side of handkerchief, 10 ch, 1 dbl tr into last dbl tr, 1 ch, turn, 1 dc into first dbl tr, 4 ch, miss 4 ch, 1 dc into next ch, 10 ch, turn, miss 1 dc, 1 dc into next dc, 1 ch, turn, 1 dc into first dc, 4 ch, miss 4 ch, 1 dc into next ch, 6 ch, turn, miss 1 dc, 1 dbl tr into next dc (corner made), 6 ch, 1 dbl tr into last dbl tr; repeat from first ★ omitting 6 ch and 1 dbl tr at end of last repeat, 1 ss into first ch worked.

dc into next loop, 3 ch) twice, 3 dc into next loop; repeat from ★ ending with 1 ss into first dc. Fasten off.

Damp and pin out to measurements.

Oversew neatly to edge of handkerchief.

Handbag

Coats ❀ Mercer-Crochet No. 20 (20 grm).
8 balls. This model is worked in shade 579 (Dark Brown), but any other shade of Mercer-Crochet may be used.
Milward steel crochet hooks 1·25 (No. 3) and 2·00 (No. 1).
¾ yd fabric 36 in. wide for lining.
½ yd Interlining.
2 Snap Fasteners.

Tension 7 patterns = 3 in.
Measurements Width 10 in.
             Depth 12 in.
             Gusset 11¼ in. × 1 in.

Main piece

Using 1·25 (No. 3) hook commence with 127 ch.

1st row 1 dc into 2nd ch from hook, 1 dc into each of the following ch, 4 ch, turn.

2nd row (right side) Miss first dc, 1 dbl tr into each of next 3 dc, ★ 1 ch, miss 1 dc, 6 dbl tr into next dc, remove loop from hook, insert hook into first dbl tr of group and draw dropped loop through, 1 ch to fasten (popcorn stitch made), 1 ch, miss 1 dc, 1 dbl tr into each of next 2 dc; repeat from ★ 23 times more, 1 dbl tr into each of next 2 sts, 2 ch, turn.

3rd row Miss first dbl tr, 1 dc into each of next 3 dbl tr, ★ 1 dc into next sp, 1 dc into top of next popcorn st, 1 dc into next sp, 1 dc into each of next 2 dbl tr; repeat from ★ 23 times more, 1 dc into each of next 2 sts, 4 ch, turn.

Repeat last 2 rows twice more.

8th row Miss first dc, ★★ thread over hook twice, insert hook into next st and draw thread through, thread over hook and draw through 2 loops, thread over hook, miss 2 sts, insert hook into next st and draw thread through, ★ thread over hook and draw through 2 loops; repeat from ★ 3 times more, 2 ch, 1 tr into centre point of cross (cross completed), 1 dbl tr into next st; repeat from ★★ to end, 4 ch, turn.

9th row Miss first dbl tr, ★ 1 cross over cross, 1 dbl tr into next dbl tr; repeat from ★ working last dbl tr into 4th of 4 ch, 4 ch, turn.

10th row As last row turning with 2 ch.

11th row Miss first dbl tr, 1 dc into next st, 2 dc into next sp, 1 dc into each of next 3 sts; repeat from ★ omitting 1 dc at end of last repeat, 4 ch, turn.
Repeat 2nd to 11th row 4 times more, then 2nd to 10th row again.
Repeat 9th row 5 times more, then repeat 10th and 11th rows. (Centre 3 rows of crosses forms base).
Repeat 2nd to 11th row 7 times more, turning with 1 ch at end of last repeat.

Flap shaping

1st row Miss first dc, 1 hlf tr into next dc, 1 tr into next dc, 1 dbl tr into next dc, continue in pattern until last popcorn st has been worked, 1 ch, miss 1 dc, 1 dbl tr into next dc, 1 tr into next dc, 1 hlf tr into next dc, 1 dc into next st, turn.

2nd row 1 ss into each of first 4 sts and into sp, continue in pattern ending with 1 dc into last popcorn st, 1 ch, turn.
Repeat last 2 rows twice more. Fasten off.

Edging

With right side facing attach thread into first of foundation ch and work a row of dc evenly all round ending with 1 ss into first dc. Fasten off.

Pocket

Commence with 127 ch.

1st row As first row of main piece.
Repeat 8th to 11th row, then 2nd to 11th row turning with 1 ch at end of last row.

Shaping

As Flap Shaping, working edging to correspond.

Gusset (make 2)

Commence with 15 ch.

1st row 1 dbl tr into 5th ch from hook, 1 dbl tr into each remaining ch, 4 ch, turn.

2nd row Miss first dbl tr, 1 dbl tr, into each of next 10 dbl tr, 1 dbl tr into 4th of 4 ch, 4 ch, turn.

Repeat last row until work measures 12 in. Fasten off.

Handle

Using double thread and 2·00 (No. 1) hook, commence with 11 ch, join with a ss to form a ring.

1st row 1 dc into same place as ss, 1 dc into each ch.

Now work in continuous rows of dc working round stem of each dc until work measures 26 in. or length required. Fasten off.

Damp and pin out to measurements.

To make up

Crochet Section. Sew gussets neatly to main section.

Lining

Using crochet for shape cut 1 piece of interlining 27 in.× 10 in. approx. for main section, 2 pieces 11¼ in.× 1 in. approx. for gussets and 1 piece 10 in.× 4 in. approx. for pocket.

Now using interlining as shape and leaving ¼ in. seam allowance all round, cut 2 pieces of lining for main section, 4 pieces for gussets and 2 pieces for pocket.

Pocket

With right sides of lining together, baste and stitch ¼ in. from edge across shaped edge and 2 short ends. Turn to right side, press and insert interlining. Turn in raw edges of open end and slipstitch neatly. Make up Main Section and Gussets to correspond.

Commencing at straight edge of main section, baste gussets in position and oversew neatly. Place lining to wrong side of crochet, sew neatly round flap and along gusset seams.

Place lining to wrong side of crochet pocket and sew neatly to edges. Place pocket in position, having shaped edge towards base of bag and sew neatly. Sew on snap fasteners and handle.

Blouse with set-in sleeves

Blouse with set-in sleeves

Coats ⚙ Mercer-Crochet No. 2 (20 grm).
12 (13, 13) balls. This model is worked in shade 439 (Rose Madder), but any other shade of Mercer-Crochet may be used.
Milward steel Crochet hooks 1·25 (No. 3), 1·50 (No. 2½).

Tension 2 patterns = 1⅜ in.
Measurements

To fit bust size	All round at underarms	Length from shoulder	Sleeve seam
32–33 in.	34½ in.	19½ in.	2½ in.
34 in.	35½ in.	20 in.	2½ in.
36 in.	38½ in.	20½ in.	2½ in.

Back and front (both alike)

Using 1·50 (No. 2½) hook commence with 202 (210, 226) ch, to measure 18 (19, 20) in. approx.

1st row 1 dc into 2nd ch from hook, ★ 4 ch, miss 3 ch, 1 dc into next ch; repeat from ★ to end, turn.

2nd row Draw loop on hook up ⅜ in., thread over hook, insert hook into first dc and draw loop up ⅜ in., (thread over hook, insert hook into same st and draw loop up as before) twice, thread over hook and draw through all loops on hook, 1 ch to fasten (making top of a 3 loop puff st), ★ 3 ch, 1 dc into the next loop, 1 dc into next dc, 1 dc into next loop, 3 ch, thread over hook, insert hook into next dc and draw loop up as before, (thread over hook, insert hook into same st and draw loop up as before) 5 times, thread over and draw through all loops on hook, 1 ch to fasten (a 6 loop puff st made); repeat from ★ omitting a 6 loop puff st at end of last repeat, a 3 loop puff st into last dc, 1 ch, turn.

3rd row 1 dc into first puff st, ★ 4 ch, miss next dc, 1 dc into next dc, 4 ch, 1 dc into next puff st; repeat from ★ ending with 1 ch, turn.

4th row 1 dc into first dc, ★ 1 dc into next loop, 3 ch, a 6 loop puff st into next dc, 3 ch, 1 dc into next loop, 1 dc into next dc; repeat from ★ ending with 1 ch, turn.

5th row 1 dc into first dc, ★ 4 ch, 1 dc into next puff st, 4 ch, miss next dc, 1 dc into next dc; repeat from ★ to end, turn.
2nd to 5th row forms the pattern.
Repeat pattern 17 times more, then 2nd to 4th row again or length required ending with a 4th pattern row, omitting turning ch at end of last row.

Armhole shaping

1st row 1 ss into each of first 11 sts, 1 dc into same place as last ss, ★ 4 ch, 1 dc into next puff st, 4 ch, miss next dc, 1 dc into next dc; repeat from ★ to within last 20 sts, 4 ch, 1 dc into next puff st, miss next dc, 1 dbl tr into next dc, 1 ch, turn.

2nd row 1 dc into first dc, 1 dc into next loop, 3 ch, continue in pattern to within last 6 sts, 1 dc into next dc, 1 ch, turn.

3rd row 1 dc into first dc, 4 ch, continue in pattern to last puff st, miss next dc, 1 dbl tr into next dc, 1 ch, turn.

Repeat last 2 rows 2 (3, 4) times more, then 2nd row again.

Now continue in pattern for 19 (23, 23) rows, or length required ending with a 5th pattern row.

Neck shaping (first side)

1st row A 3 loop puff st into first dc, ★ 3 ch, 1 dc into next loop, 1 dc into next dc, 1 dc into next loop, 3 ch, a 6 loop puff st into next dc; repeat from ★ 5 times more, 3 ch, 1 dc into next loop, 1 dc into next dc, 5 ch, turn.

2nd row 1 dc into first puff st, 4 ch, continue in pattern to end.

3rd row Work in pattern to last dc, 5 ch, turn.

Repeat last 2 rows 5 times more then 2nd row again.

Work in pattern for 5 rows ending at neck edge. Fasten off.

Shoulder shaping

1st row Work in pattern to last puff st, 1 dbl tr into next dc, turn.

2nd row 1 dc into first dc, 3 ch, pattern to end, 1 ch, turn.

3rd row 1 dc into puff st, 4 ch, miss next dc, 1 dc into next dc, 4 ch, 1 dc into next puff st, miss next dc, 1 dbl tr into next dc, turn.

4th row 1 dc into first dc, 1 dc into next loop, pattern to end, 1 ch, turn.

5th row 1 dc into first dc, 4 ch, 1 dc into puff st, 4 ch, miss next dc, 1 dc into next dc. Fasten off.

Neck shaping (second side)

1st row Miss 11 (11, 13) dc, attach thread to next dc, 1 dc into same place as join, 1 dc into next loop, 3 ch, continue in pattern to end.

2nd row Work in pattern to within last puff st, 4 ch, 1 dc into puff st, 5 ch, turn.

3rd row Miss first dc, a 6 loop puff st into next dc, 3 ch, continue in pattern to end. Repeat last 2 rows 5 times more, then 2nd row again.

Work in pattern for 5 rows turning with 4 ch at end of last row (sleeve edge).

Shoulder shaping

1st row 1 dc into first puff st, 4 ch, pattern to end, 1 ch, turn.

2nd row Work in pattern ending with 1 dbl tr into last dc, turn.

3rd row 1 ss into each of first 7 sts, 4 ch, pattern to end.

4th row 1 dc into first dc, 3 ch, miss next dc, a 6 loop puff st into next dc, 1 dbl tr into next dc, 4 ch, turn.

5th row 1 dc into puff st, 4 ch, 1 dc into next dc. Fasten off.

Sleeves (both alike)

Using 1·50 (No. 2½) hook commence with 138 (146, 154) ch and work as Back for 8 rows, omitting turning ch at end of last row.

Shape top

1st row As 1st row of Armhole Shaping.

2nd row Work in pattern to within last 11 sts, 3 ch, a 6 loop puff st into next dc, 1 dbl tr into next dc, 1 ch, turn.

3rd row Work in pattern to within last puff st, 4 ch, 1 dc into puff st, miss next dc, 1 dbl tr into next dc.

4th row Work in pattern.
Work in pattern for 4 rows more.

9th row Work in pattern to within last puff st, 4 ch, 1 dc into puff st, miss next dc, 1 dbl tr into next dc.

10th row Work in pattern to within last 6 sts, 1 dc into next dc, 1 ch, turn.
Work in pattern for 4 rows more.

15th row Work in pattern to within last puff st, 4 ch, 1 dc into puff st, miss next dc, 1 dbl tr into next dc, 1 ch, turn.

16th row Work in pattern to within last 11 sts, 3 ch, 1 puff st into next dc, 1 dbl tr into next dc, 1 ch, turn.
Repeat last 2 rows 6 times more, then 15th row again. Fasten off.

To make up

Sew side, shoulder and sleeve seams. Sew sleeves into armholes.

Lower edging

1st row Attach thread to side seam and using 1·25 (No. 3) hook, work a row of dc over foundation ch having a multiple of 3 dc.

2nd to 4th row 1 dc into each dc, ending 4th row with 1 ss into first dc.

5th row Draw loop on hook up ⅜ in. and complete a 6 loop puff st, ★ 2 ch, miss 2 dc, a 6 loop puff st into next dc; repeat from ★ ending with 2 ch, 1 ss into first puff st.

6th row 1 dc into same place as ss ★ 2 dc into sp, 1 dc into next puff st; repeat from ★ ending with 2 dc into last sp.

7th to 9th row 1 dc into each dc, ending 9th row with 1 ss into first dc. Fasten off.

Sleeve edging

Attach thread to seam and complete as Lower Edging.

Neck edging

Attach thread to shoulder seam and work as Lower Edging for 5 rows.

6th row 2 dc into each sp.

7th to 9th row As 7th to 9th row of Lower Edging.

Damp and pin out to measurements.

Motif blouse

Coats ⚬ Mercer-Crochet No. 20 (20 grm).

12 balls No. 20 to fit Bust 38–40 in.

Milward steel crochet hook No. 3 (1·25 mm).

8 balls No. 40 to fit Bust 34–36 in.

Milward steel crochet hook 1·00 (No. 4).

This model is worked in shade 624 (Blush Pink), but any other shade of Mercer-Crochet may be used.

Tension Size of motif

No. 20 = $1\frac{3}{4}$ in. in diameter.

No. 40 = $1\frac{1}{2}$ in. in diameter.

Measurements

Bust 38–40 in.

Length from shoulder 21 in.

Bust 34–36 in.

Length from shoulder 19 in.

Motif

Commence with 6 ch, join with a ss to form a ring.

1st row 5 ch, ★ 1 tr into ring, 2 ch; repeat from ★ 4 times more, 1 ss into 3rd of 5 ch. (6 sps).

2nd row 4 ch, 2 dbl tr into same place as last ss, ★ 2 ch, 1 dbl tr into next sp, 3 ch, 1 ss into top of last dbl tr (picot made), 2 ch, 3 dbl tr into next tr; repeat from ★ omitting 3 dbl tr at end of last repeat, 1 ss into 4th of 4 ch.

3rd row 4 ch, 1 dbl tr into same place as last ss, ★ 1 dbl tr into next dbl tr, 2 dbl tr into next dbl tr, 3 ch, 1 dc 4 ch and 1 dc into next picot, 3 ch, 2 dbl tr into next dbl tr; repeat from ★ omitting 2 dbl tr at end of last repeat, 1 ss into 4th of 4 ch. Fasten off.

Half motif

Commence with 6 ch, join with a ss to form a ring.

1st row 5 ch, ★ 1 tr into ring, 2 ch; repeat from ★ twice more, 1 tr into ring, 1 ch, turn.

2nd row 1 ss into first sp, 7 ch, 1 ss into 4th ch from hook, 2 ch, (3 dbl tr into next tr, 2 ch, 1 dbl tr into next sp, 3 ch, 1 ss into top of last dbl tr, 2 ch) twice, 3 dbl tr into next tr, 2 ch, 1 dbl tr into next sp, 3 ch, 1 ss into top of last dbl tr, 1 ch, turn.

3rd row 1 dc into first picot, (3 ch, 2 dbl tr into next dbl tr, 1 dbl tr into next dbl tr, 2 dbl tr into next dbl tr, 3 ch, 1 dc 4 ch and 1 dc into next picot) twice, 3 ch, 2 dbl tr into next dbl tr, 1 dbl tr into next dbl tr, 2 dbl tr into next dbl tr, 3 ch, 1 dc into next picot. Fasten off.

Back

Make 186 motifs and 6 half motifs.

The motifs are sewn together by the groups of 5 dbl tr. Sew the rows of motifs from left to right.

1st row Sew 12 motifs in a straight line.

2nd row Sew 11 motifs as before. Now join first motif to first motif of row 1 by 5 dbl tr group before join and to 5 dbl tr group on second motif of row 1 by 5 dbl tr group after join. The second motif of this row will be joined by 3 dbl tr groups (i.e. to first group of third motif also). All motifs are joined in this way. See illustration.

3rd row 10 motifs, making first join as row 2.

At each end of this row sew a half motif thus: place centre of straight edge to centre of first 5 dbl tr group of first motif and sew together. Now sew side of end sp of half motif to 5 dbl tr group of first motif on row 2. Sew a half motif at end of this row to correspond.

4th row 11 motifs, joining first motif to side of top sp of half motif.

5th row 12 motifs, joining first motif to second 5 dbl tr group before joining on row 4 (1 join only) thus increasing for shaping.

6th row 13 motifs, first join as row 5.

7th row 12 motifs, first join as row 2.

8th row 13 motifs, first join as row 5.

Armhole shaping

9th row 12 motifs, first join as row 2.

10th row With straight edge facing right, sew 1 half motif by lower 5 dbl tr group to second 5 dbl tr group before join of previous row. Next motif, sew a picot to top dbl tr on edge of half motif, slip cotton to dbl tr group of motif and sew to centre of half motif, slip cotton to next picot and sew to base of dc on half motif, slip cotton to next group on motif, continue joining 10 more motifs and 1 half motif at end of row to correspond with half motif at beginning of row, having straight edge of half motif facing left.

11th row 12 motifs, making first join to half motif, slip cotton to dc on half motif and join to next picot, slip cotton to next 5 dbl tr group of motif and join to 5 dbl tr group of motif of previous row. Join last motif to half motif to correspond.

12th row 13 motifs, first join as row 5 (to increase).

13th row 14 motifs, first join as row 5.

14th row 13 motifs, first join as row 2 (shoulder shaping).

15th row 10 motifs, miss first motif of previous row and join to second and third motif as for row 2.

16th row 7 motifs, joining as on last row.

17th row Join a half motif to first 2 motifs of row 16 thus: with straight edge facing downwards and sewing from left, sew last dc to second picot above first join of previous row, slip cotton down side of 2 sps on half motif and sew to first dbl tr of group, sew centre of half motif to 4 dbl tr of same group, slip cotton to first dc on half motif, and sew to first picot of next motif in previous row, slip cotton to 5 dbl tr group of half motif and sew to 5 dbl tr group of motif. Sew half motif in corresponding position at other end of this row.

Front

Make 159 motifs and 6 half motifs.

1st row Join 10 motifs in a straight line.

2nd row 11 motifs, first join as row 5 of back (to increase).

3rd row 10 motifs, first join as row 2 of back.

4th row 11 motifs, first join as row 5 of back.

5th row 10 motifs, first join as row 2 of back, at each end of this row join a half motif thus: with straight edge facing right, sew last dc to first picot on left of first motif, slip cotton to next row on half motif and sew to first dbl tr of next 5 dbl tr group, sew next 2 sps to 4 dbl tr, slip cotton to centre of half motif and sew centre to next picot on motif, sew remaining half of motif to correspond, sew other half motif at end of row to correspond.

6th row 11 motifs, making first join to 5 dbl tr group at top of half motif (one join only).

7th row Join first motif to third 5 dbl tr group to left of joining between first and second motifs on 6th row. Now join a half motif thus: with straight edge facing left, sew first dc on right of half motif to second picot above join of first and second motifs of previous row, slip cotton to base of picot on half motif and sew to first dbl tr of group on same motif, sew row-end to remaining 4 dbl tr of same group, slip cotton across centre of half motif and sew next row-end and base of picot to 5 dbl tr group on first motif of row 7. Next motif, join to lower group of 5 dbl tr of half motif and corresponding groups to row 6. Join 9 more motifs. Now sew a half motif and the 12th motif to correspond with beginning of row.

8th row 13 motifs, joining first motif to 5 dbl tr group to left of first join on row 7, and the next 5 dbl tr group to 5 dbl tr group of half motif. Sew end of row to correspond.

9th row 12 motifs, first join as row 2 of back (shoulder shaping).

10th row As row 10 of back.

11th row As row 11 of back.

12th row 6 motifs only (for shoulder shaping and neck opening) making first join as row 5 of back (to increase). Join first motif between 7th and 8th motifs of row 11. Join remaining rows to correspond. Sew up shoulder and side motifs, joining corresponding groups of dbl tr.

13th row 6 motifs as last row.

14th row 4 motifs, joining first motif between second and third motifs of last row.

15th row 2 motifs, joining as on last row.

Other shoulder and neck opening.

Edging

Round lower edge of blouse.

1st row Attach thread to centre picot on any motif, * 1 dc into picot, 3 ch, 1 dc into next sp, 3 ch, 1 dc into centre dbl tr of 5 dbl tr group, 3 ch, 1 dc into next sp, 3 ch, 1 dc into each of next 2 picots, 3 ch, 1 dc into next sp, 3 ch, 1 dc into centre dbl tr of 5 dbl tr groups, 3 ch, 1 dc into next sp, 3 ch; repeat from * all round, 1 ss into first dc.

2nd row 1 ch, * (1 dc into next sp, 3 ch, 1 dc into top of last dc—picot made—1 dc into same sp) 3 times, 1 dc

into next sp, picot, 1 dc into next sp, (1 dc picot and 1 dc into next sp) 3 times; repeat from * all round. Fasten off.

Work first row of this edging round neck edge but where the half motifs occur and only one dbl tr group on each side of half motif do not join the 2 picots together and work thus: 1 dc into picot, 3 ch, (1 dc into next sp) twice, 3 ch, 1 dc into next picot and continue. Work 2nd row of edging to correspond.

This method applies to the armholes with this exception: join the 2 picots together at base of armhole.

Damp and press.

Tailored blouse

Coats ⚙ Mercer-Crochet No. 20 (20 grm).
10 (11, 12) balls. This model is worked in White, but any shade of Mercer-Crochet may be used.
Milward steel crochet hook 1·25 (No. 3).
5 buttons.

Tension
5 rows of tr = 1 in.
10 tr = 1 in.

Measurements

To fit bust size	Actual measurements	Length from shoulder	Sleeve seam
34 in.	36 in.	18 in.	4 in.
36 in.	38 in.	19 in.	4 in.
38 in.	40 in.	20 in.	4 in.

Back

Basque

Commence with 157 (167, 177) ch.

1st row 1 tr into 4th ch from hook, 1 tr into each ch, 3 ch, turn.

2nd to 6th row Miss first tr, 1 tr into each tr, 1 tr into 3rd of 3 ch, 3 ch, turn.

Main section

1st row Miss first tr, 1 tr into each of next 14 (19, 24) tr, ★ 3 ch, miss 2 tr, 1 dc into next tr, 3 ch, miss 2 tr, 1 tr into each of next 19 tr; repeat from ★ 4 times more, 3 ch, miss 2 tr, 1 dc into next tr, 3 ch, miss 2 tr, 1 tr into each of next 15 (20, 25) sts, 3 ch, turn.

2nd row Miss first tr, 1 tr into each of next 12 (17, 22) tr, ★ 3 ch, 1 dc into next loop, 5 ch, 1 dc into next loop, 3 ch, miss 2 tr, 1 tr into each of next 15 tr; repeat from ★ 4 times more, 3 ch, 1 dc into next loop, 5 ch, 1 dc into next loop, 3 ch, miss 2 tr, 1 tr into each of next 13 (18, 23) sts, 3 ch, turn.

3rd row Miss first tr, 1 tr into each of next 10 (15, 20) tr, ★ 3 ch, 1 dc into next loop, 5 ch, 3 dc into next loop, 5 ch, 1 dc into next loop, 3 ch, miss 2 tr, 1 tr into each of next 11 tr; repeat from ★ 4 times more, 3 ch, 1 dc into next loop, 5 ch, 3 dc into next loop, 5 ch, 1 dc into next loop, 3 ch, miss 2 tr, 1 tr into each of next 11 (16, 21) sts, 3 ch, turn.

4th row Miss first tr, 1 tr into each of next 8 (13, 18) tr, ★ 3 ch, 1 dc into next loop, (5 ch, 3 dc into next loop) twice, 5 ch, 1 dc into next loop, miss 2 tr, 1 tr into each of next 7 tr; repeat from ★ 4 times more, 3 ch, 1 dc into next loop, (5 ch, 3 dc into next loop) twice, 5 ch, 1 dc into next loop, miss 2 tr, 1 tr into each of next 9 (14, 19) sts, 3 ch, turn.

5th row Miss first tr, 1 tr into each of next 8 (13, 18) tr, ★ 2 tr into next loop, 3 ch, 1 dc into next loop, 5 ch, 3 dc into next loop, 5 ch, 1 dc into next loop, 3 ch, 2 tr into next loop, 1 tr into each of next 7 tr; repeat from ★ 4 times more, 2 tr into next loop, 3 ch, 1 dc into next loop, 5 ch, 3 dc into next loop, 5 ch, 1 dc into next loop, 3 ch, 2 tr into next loop, 1 tr into each of next 9 (14, 19) sts, 3 ch, turn.

6th row Miss first tr, 1 tr into each of next 10 (15, 20) tr, ★ 2 tr into next loop, 3 ch, 1 dc into next loop, 5 ch, 1 dc into next loop, 3 ch, 2 tr into next loop, 1 tr into each of next 11 tr; repeat from ★ 4 times more, 2 tr into next loop, 3 ch, 1 dc into next loop, 5 ch, 1 dc into next loop, 3 ch, 2 tr into next loop, 1 tr into each of next 11 (16, 21) sts, 3 ch, turn.

7th row Miss first tr, 1 tr into each of next 12 (17, 22) tr, ★ 2 tr into next loop, 3 ch, 1 dc into next loop, 3 ch, 2 tr into next loop, 1 tr into each of next 15 tr; repeat from ★ 4 times more, 2 tr into next loop, 3 ch, 1 dc into next loop, 3 ch, 2 tr into next loop, 1 tr into each of next 13 (18, 23) sts, 3 ch, turn.
2nd to 7th row forms pattern.

8th row (increase) 1 tr into first tr (increase made at beginning of row), work in pattern to last tr, 2 tr into 3rd of 3 ch (increase made at end of row), 3 ch, turn.

9th row Miss first tr, 1 tr into each of next 11 (16, 21) tr, 3 ch, work in pattern ending with 1 tr into each of next 12 (17, 22) sts, 3 ch, turn.

Continue in pattern increasing 1 st at each end of next and every alternate row until 17 increases in all have been worked.
Continue in pattern over these sts for 4 (10, 16) rows more omitting turning ch at end of last row.

Armhole shaping

1st row 1 ss into each of first 14 sts, 3 ch, work in pattern to within last 13 sts, 3 ch, turn.

112

2nd row Miss first st, leaving the last loop of each on hook work 1 tr into each of next 2 tr, thread over and draw through all loops on hook (a joint tr made), work in pattern to within last 3 sts, a joint tr over next 2 sts, 1 tr into 3rd of 3 ch, 3 ch, turn.

3rd row Miss first tr, a joint tr over next 2 sts, work in pattern to within last tr, a joint tr over next 2 sts, 1 tr into 3rd of 3 ch, 3 ch, turn.

Repeat last row 2 (4, 6) times more.
Continue in pattern over these sts for 30 (28, 26) rows more.

Next row Miss first tr, 1 tr into each of next 14 (17, 20) tr, ★ 2 tr into next loop, 1 tr into next dc, 2 tr into next loop, 1 tr into each of next 19 tr; repeat from ★ 4 times more, 2 tr into next loop, 1 tr into next dc, 2 tr into next loop, 1 tr into each of next 15 (18, 21) sts, turn.

Shoulder shaping

1st and 2nd rows 1 ss into each of first 14 sts, 1 ch, 1 dc into each of next 2 tr, 1 hlf tr into each of next 3 tr, 1 tr into each tr to within last 19 sts, 1 hlf tr into each of next 3 tr, 1 dc into each of next 3 tr, turn.

3rd and 4th rows 1 ss into first 13 sts, 1 ch, 1 dc into each of next 2 tr, 1 hlf tr into each of next 3 tr, 1 tr into each tr to within last 18 sts, 1 hlf tr into each of next 3 tr, 1 dc into each of next 3 dc, turn. Fasten off.

Right front

Basque

Commence with 98 (103, 108) ch and work as Back for 3 rows.

4th row Miss first tr, 1 tr into each tr to within last 13 sts, 5 ch, miss 5 tr, 1 tr into each of next 8 sts (buttonhole made), 3 ch, turn.

5th row Miss first tr, 1 tr into each of next 7 tr, 1 tr into each of next 5 ch, 1 tr into each st, 3 ch, turn.

6th row Miss first tr, 1 tr into each st, 3 ch, turn.

Main section

1st row Miss first tr, 1 tr into each of next 27 tr, ★ 3 ch, miss 2 tr, 1 dc into next tr, 3 ch, miss 2 tr, 1 tr into each of next 19 tr; repeat from ★ once more, 3 ch, miss 2 tr, 1 dc into next tr, 3 ch, miss 2 tr, 1 tr into each of next 15 (20, 25) sts, 3 ch, turn.

2nd row Miss first tr, 1 tr into each of next 12 (17, 22) tr, ★ 3 ch, 1 dc into next loop, 5 ch, 1 dc into next loop, 3 ch, miss 2 tr, 1 tr into each of next 15 tr; repeat from ★ once more, 3 ch, 1 dc into next loop, 5 ch, 1 dc into next loop, 3 ch, miss 2 tr, 1 tr into each of next 26 sts, 3 ch, turn.

3rd row Miss first tr, 1 tr into each of next 23 tr, ★ 3 ch, 1 dc into next loop, 5 ch, 3 dc into next loop, 5 ch, 1 dc into next loop, 3 ch, miss 2 tr, 1 tr into each of next 11 tr; repeat from ★ once more, 3 ch, 1 dc into next loop, 5 ch, 3 dc into next loop, 5 ch, 1 dc into next loop, 3 ch, miss 2 tr, 1 tr into each of next 11 (16, 21) sts, 3 ch, turn.

4th row Miss first tr, 1 tr into each of next 8 (13, 18) tr, ★ 3 ch, 1 dc into next loop (5 ch, 3 dc into next loop) twice, 5 ch, 1 dc into next loop, 3 ch, miss 2 tr, 1 tr into each of next 7 tr; repeat from ★ once more, 3 ch, 1 dc into next loop (5 ch, 3 dc into next loop) twice, 5 ch, 1 dc into next loop, 3 ch, miss 2 tr, 1 tr into each of next 22 sts, 3 ch, turn.

5th row Miss first tr, 1 tr into each of next 21 tr, 2 tr into next loop, ★ 3 ch, 1 dc into next loop, 5 ch, 3 dc into next loop, 5 ch, 1 dc into next loop, 3 ch, 2 tr into next loop, 1 tr into each of next 7 tr; repeat from ★ once more, 2 tr into next loop, 3 ch, 1 dc into next loop, 5 ch, 3 dc into next loop, 5 ch, 1 dc into next loop, 3 ch, 2 tr into next loop, 1 tr into each of next 9 (14, 19) sts, 3 ch, turn.

6th row Miss first tr, 1 tr into each of next 10 (15, 20) tr, ★ 2 tr into next loop, 3 ch, 1 dc into next loop, 5 ch, 1 dc into next loop, 3 ch, 2 tr into next loop, 1 tr into each of next 11 tr; repeat from ★ once more, 2 tr into next loop, 3 ch, 1 dc into next loop, 5 ch, 1 dc into next loop, 3 ch, 2 tr into next loop, 1 tr into each of next 24 sts, 3 ch, turn.

7th row Miss first tr, 1 tr into each of next 25 tr, ★ 2 tr into next loop, 3 ch, 1 dc into next loop, 3 ch, 2 tr into next loop, 1 tr into each of next 15 tr; repeat from ★ once more, 2 tr into next loop, 3 ch, 1 dc into next loop, 3 ch, 2 tr into next loop, 1 tr into each of next 13 (18, 23) sts, 3 ch, turn. 2nd to 7th row forms pattern.

Continue in pattern, increasing 1 st at beginning of next and every alternate row until 17 increases in all have been worked and working a buttonhole on every 12th row from previous buttonhole until 4 (5, 5) buttonholes in all have been worked. Continue in pattern over these sts for 4 (10, 16) rows more.

Armhole shaping

1st size only

1st row Work in pattern to within last 13 sts, 3 ch, turn.

2nd row Miss first tr, a joint tr over next 2 sts, work in pattern to within last 13 sts, 5 ch, miss 5 tr, 1 tr into each of next 8 sts, 3 ch, turn.

3rd row Work in pattern to within last tr, a joint tr over next 2 sts, 1 tr into 3rd of 3 ch, 3 ch, turn.
Repeat last 2 rows once more omitting buttonhole.

2nd and 3rd sizes only

1st row Work in pattern to within last 13 sts, 3 ch, turn.

2nd row Miss first tr, a joint tr over next 2 sts, work in pattern to end of row.

3rd row Work in pattern to within last tr, a joint tr over next 2 sts, 1 tr into 3rd of 3 ch, 3 ch, turn.
Repeat last 2 rows 2 (3) times more.

All sizes

Continue in pattern over these sts for 12 (10, 8) rows more.

Next row Miss first tr, 1 tr into each of next 12 (15, 18) tr, 3 ch, 1 dc into next loop, 5 ch, 1 dc into next loop, 3 ch, miss 2 tr, 1 tr into each of next 15 tr, 3 ch, 1 dc into next loop, 5 ch, 1 dc into next loop, 3 ch, miss 2 tr, 1 tr into each of next 17 tr, 2 tr into next loop, 1 tr into next dc, 2 tr into next loop, 1 tr into each of next 28 sts, 3 ch, turn.

Next row Miss first tr, 1 tr into each of next 47 tr, 3 ch, 1 dc into next loop, 5 ch, 3 dc into next loop, 5 ch, 1 dc into next loop, 3 ch, miss 2 tr, 1 tr into each of next 11 tr, 3 ch, 1 dc into next loop, 5 ch, 3 dc into next loop, 5 ch, 1 dc into next loop, 3 ch, miss 2 tr, 1 tr into each of next 11 (14, 17) sts, 3 ch, turn.
Continue in pattern over these sts for 7 rows more, omitting turning ch at end of last row.

Neck shaping

1st row 1 ss into first 39 sts, 3 ch, 1 tr into

each of next 7 tr, 2 tr into next loop, work in pattern to end of row.

2nd row Work in pattern to within last 3 sts, a joint tr over next 2 sts, 1 tr into 3rd of 3 ch, 3 ch, turn.

3rd row Miss first tr, a joint tr over next 2 sts, work in pattern to end of row.
Repeat last 2 rows twice more.
Continue in pattern over these sts for 2 rows more.

Next row Miss first tr, 1 tr into each of next 14 (17, 20) tr, 2 tr into next loop, 1 tr into next dc, 2 tr into next loop, 1 tr into each of next 19 tr, 2 tr into next loop, 1 tr into next dc, 2 tr into next loop, 1 tr into each of next 8 sts, 3 ch, turn.

Shoulder shaping

1st row Work in pattern to within last 18 sts, 1 hlf tr into each of next 3 tr, 1 dc into each of next 3 tr, turn.

2nd row 1 ss into each of first 14 sts, 1 ch, 1 dc into each of next 2 tr, 1 hlf tr into each of next 3 tr, 1 tr into each st, 3 ch, turn.

3rd row Work in pattern to within last 17 sts, 1 hlf tr into each of next 3 tr, 1 dc into each of next 3 tr. Fasten off.

Left front

Basque

Commence with 98 (103, 108) ch and work as Back for 6 rows.

Main section

1st row Miss first tr, 1 tr into each of next 14 (19, 24) tr, ★ 3 ch, miss 2 tr, 1 dc into next tr, 3 ch, miss 2 tr, 1 tr into each of next 19 tr; repeat from ★ once more, 3 ch, miss 2 tr, 1 dc into next tr, 3 ch, miss 2 tr, 1 tr into each of next 28 sts, 3 ch, turn.

2nd row Miss first tr, 1 tr into each of next 25 tr, ★ 3 ch, 1 dc into next loop, 5 ch, 1 dc into next loop, 3 ch, miss 2 tr, 1 tr into each of next 15 tr; repeat from ★ once more, 3 ch, 1 dc into next loop, 5 ch, 1 dc into next loop, 3 ch, miss 2 tr, 1 tr into each of next 13 (18, 23) sts, 3 ch, turn.
Complete to correspond with Right Front omitting buttonholes.

Sleeves

Commence with 133 ch and work as Back for 4 rows.

5th row Miss first tr, 1 tr into each of next 14 tr, ★ 3 ch, miss 2 tr, 1 dc into next tr, 3 ch, miss 2 tr, 1 tr into each of next 19 tr; repeat from ★ 3 times more, 3 ch, miss 2 tr, 1 dc into next tr, 3 ch, miss 2 tr, 1 tr into each of next 15 sts, 3 ch, turn.

6th row Miss first tr, 1 tr into each of next 12 tr, ★ 3 ch, 1 dc into next loop, 5 ch, 1 dc into next loop, 3 ch, miss 2 tr, 1 tr into each of next 15 tr; repeat from ★ 3 times more, 3 ch, 1 dc into next loop, 5 ch, 1 dc into next loop, 3 ch, miss 2 tr, 1 tr into each of next 13 sts, 3 ch, turn.

Continue in pattern over these sts for 2 rows more.

Continue in pattern increasing 1 st at each end of next and every alternate row until 6 increases in all have been worked.

Next row Work in pattern, omitting turning ch at end of row.

Shape top

1st row 1 ss into each of first 14 sts, 3 ch, work in pattern to within last 13 sts, 3 ch, turn.

2nd row Miss first tr, a joint tr over next 2 sts, work in pattern to within last 3 sts, a joint tr over next 2 sts, 1 tr into 3rd of 3 ch, 3 ch, turn.

Repeat last row twice more.

5th row Miss first tr, a joint tr over next 2 sts, 5 ch, 3 dc into next 5 ch loop, work in pattern to within last 2 loops, 3 dc into next loop, 5 ch, miss 1 loop, a joint tr over next 2 sts, 1 tr into 3rd of 3 ch, 5 ch, turn.

6th row 3 dc into first loop, work in pattern to within last loop, 3 dc into next loop, 2 ch, 1 tr into 3rd of 3 ch, 5 ch, turn.

7th row Miss first loop, 3 dc into next loop, work in pattern to within last 2 loops, 3 dc into next loop, 2 ch, 1 tr into 3rd of 5 ch, 6 ch, turn.

8th row Miss first loop, 1 dc into next loop, work in pattern to within last 2 loops, 1 dc into next loop, 3 ch, 1 tr into 3rd of 5 ch, 4 ch, turn.

9th row Miss first loop, 2 tr into next loop, work in pattern to within last 2 loops, 2 tr into last loop, 1 ch, 1 tr into 3rd of 6 ch, 3 ch, turn.

10th row Miss first 3 tr, work in pattern to within last 2 tr, 1 tr into 3rd of 4 ch, 3 ch, turn.

11th row Miss first tr, a joint tr over next 2 tr, work in pattern to within last 3 sts, a joint tr over next 2 sts, 1 tr into 3rd of 3 ch, 3 ch, turn.

12th row Miss first tr, leaving the last loop of each on hook work 1 tr into each of next 3 sts, thread over and draw through all loops on hook (a 3 tr cluster made), work in pattern to within last 4 sts, a 3 tr cluster over next 3 sts, 1 tr into 3rd of 3 ch, 3 ch, turn.

Repeat last 2 rows twice more omitting turning ch at end of last row.

Next row 1 ss into each of first 7 sts, 1 dc into next loop, 2 ch, 3 dc into next loop, work in pattern to within last 2 loops, 3 dc into next loop, 2 ch, 1 dc into next loop, turn.

Next row 1 ss into each of next 8 sts, 3 ch, 1 dc into next loop, work in pattern to within last 3 loops, 1 dc into next loop, 1 tr into next loop, turn.

Next row 1 ss into each of first 14 sts, 2 ch, 1 dc into next loop, 3 ch, 3 dc into next loop, 3 ch, 1 dc into next loop, 2 ch, 1 ss into next loop. Fasten off.

Collar

Commence with 136 (140, 144) ch.

1st row 1 tr into 4th ch from hook, 1 tr into each ch, 3 ch, turn.

2nd to 11th row Miss first tr, 1 tr into each tr, 1 tr into 3rd of 3 ch, 3 ch, turn, omitting turning ch at end of last row.

12th row 1 ss into each of first 12 sts, 1 dc into next tr, 1 tr into each tr to within last 13 sts, 1 dc into next tr, turn.

Repeat last row twice more. Fasten off.

To make up

Sew side, shoulder and sleeve seams. Sew sleeves into armholes. Sew on buttons to correspond with buttonholes.

Damp and press.

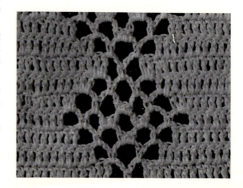

116

Bloomer set

Trimming for top and bloomer set

Coats ✻ Mercer-Crochet No. 40 (20 grm).

1 ball. This model is worked in shade 508 (Lt Marine Blue), but any other shade of Mercer-Crochet may be used.

Milward steel crochet hook 1·00 (No. 4).

A Sleeveless Top and Bloomers or $\frac{7}{8}$ yd fabric 36 in. wide and $\frac{7}{8}$ yd lining 36 in. wide.

Size of small motif $\frac{3}{4}$ in. square.
Size of large motif $1\frac{1}{2}$ in. from point to point.

Layout of Top and Bloomers to fit a 23 in. chest.

Small motif trimming

First small motif

Commence with 5 ch.

1st row Leaving the last loop of each on hook work 2 dbl tr into 5th ch from hook, thread over and draw through all loops on hook (a 2 dbl tr cluster made), (6 ch, a 3 dbl tr cluster into same ch) 3 times, 6 ch, 1 ss into first cluster.

2nd row Into each loop work 5 dc 3 ch and 5 dc, 1 ss into first dc. Fasten off.

Second small motif

Work as first motif for 1 row.

2nd row 5 dc into next loop, 1 ch, 1 dc into any 3 ch loop on first motif, 1 ch, 5 dc into same loop on second motif and complete as first motif. Make 19 more motifs or number required joining each as second motif was joined to first, placing as shown on diagram.

Large motif (make 5)

Commence with 8 ch, join with a ss to form a ring.

1st row 6 ch, (1 hlf tr into ring, 4 ch) 7 times, 1 ss into 2nd of 6 ch.

2nd row 1 ss into each of next 2 ch and into same loop, 8 ch, (1 hlf tr into next loop, 6 ch) 7 times, 1 ss into 2nd of 8 ch.

3rd row Into each loop work 5 dc 3 ch and 5 dc, 1 ss into first dc. Fasten off.

Damp and pin out to measurements.

To make up

Top

$\frac{5}{8}$ in. seam allowance has been given on all pieces.

Join side seams and press open.

Join side seams of lining and press open.

Place top and lining right sides together and stitch back edge, neck and armhole edges. Clip curves, turn to right side and press. Join shoulder seams of top and press open. Slipstitch shoulder edges of lining. Turn up hem along lower edge and slipstitch lining to hem. Work buttonholes on back and sew on buttons to correspond.

Bloomers

Join front and back seams and clip curves.
Join crutch seam.
Make up lining to correspond.
Place bloomers and lining wrong sides together. Fold waist edge to inside to form a casing and stitch leaving an opening to insert elastic.
Make casings on leg edges to correspond.
Insert elastic to fit.
Place small motif trimming centrally to front of top having lowest motif approx. 2 in. from lower edge and sew in position. Sew large motifs on each side of small motif trimming as shown in illustration.

into next dc, 1 dbl tr into centre dc of free group at corner, miss first 2 dc from joining on next motif, 1 dbl tr into next dc, thread over and draw through all loops on hook (a 3 joint dbl tr made at corner), 4 ch, 1 tr into centre dc of next group, 4 ch, 1 dc into centre dc of next group; repeat from first ★ once more, complete remaining side to correspond. Fasten off.

Damp and pin out to measurements.
Slipstitch to edge of apron.
Damp and press.

2 balls Coats ✿ Mercer-Crochet No. 20 (20 grm). A ready made Gingham apron. Milward steel crochet hook 1·25 (No. 3).

Size of motif $1\frac{3}{4}$ in. in diameter.

All over pattern bath mat

Coats 'Musica' Knitting Cotton.
2 oz Ready Wound Balls. 8 balls.
Milward Disc (aluminium) crochet hook 3·50 (No. 9).
1¼ yds Towelling, 36 in. wide.
1¼ yds light weight fabric 36 in. wide for lining.
Or Bath Mat.

Tension
2 rows = 1 in. measured over pattern.

Measurements
Size of crochet 35 in. × 22 in.
Size of mat   37 in. × 24 in.

Commence with 171 ch, to measure approx. 35 in. (a multiple of 6 ch plus 3).

1st row 1 tr into 4th ch from hook, 1 tr into each ch, 4 ch, turn.

2nd row Leaving last loop of each on hook work 2 dbl tr into first tr, thread over and draw through all loops on hook (a 2 dbl tr cluster made), ★ 3 ch, miss 2 tr, 1 dc into next tr, 3 ch, a 3 dbl tr cluster into next tr; repeat from ★ ending with 1 ch, turn.

3rd row 1 dc into first cluster, ★ 3 ch, a 3 dbl tr cluster into next dc, 3 ch, 1 dc into next cluster; repeat from ★ ending with 4 ch, turn.

4th row A 2 dbl tr cluster into first dc, ★ 3 ch, 1 dc into next cluster, 3 ch, a 3 dbl tr cluster into next dc; repeat from ★ ending with 1 ch, turn.
Repeat 3rd and 4th rows 21 times more, ending last row with 3 ch, turn.

Last row Miss first cluster, ★ 2 tr into next sp, 1 tr into next dc, 2 tr into next sp, 1 tr into next cluster; repeat from ★ to end. Fasten off.

Damp and pin out to measurements.

To make up

Cut towelling 38 in. × 25 in. Cut lining 38 in. × 25 in. Place crochet centrally on to towelling and slipstitch in position. Place towelling and lining right sides together and machine stitch ½ in. from edges, leaving an opening sufficiently large to turn to right side. Slipstitch open edges together, or sew in position to bath mat.

Motif pattern bath mat

**Coats 'Musica' Knitting Cotton.
2 oz Ready Wound Balls. 7 balls.
Milward Disc (aluminium) crochet
hook 3·50 (No. 9).
1 yd Towelling 36 in. wide.
1 yd light weight fabric 36 in. wide for
lining.
Or Bath Mat.**

Size of motif 3 in.

Measurements
Size of crochet 18 in.× 27 in.
Size of mat   20 in.× 29 in.

First motif

Commence with 8 ch, join with a ss to
form a ring.

1st row 3 ch, leaving last loop of each on
hook work 2 tr into ring, thread over and
draw through all loops on hook (a 2 tr
cluster made), ★ 6 ch, a 3 tr cluster into
ring; repeat from ★ twice more, 6 ch, 1 ss
into first cluster.

2nd row 5 ch, ★ into next loop work 2 tr
4 ch and 2 tr, 2 ch, 1 tr into next cluster,
2 ch; repeat from ★ omitting 1 tr at end of
last repeat, 1 ss into 3rd of 5 ch.

3rd row 3 ch, ★ 2 tr into next sp, 1 tr into
each of next 2 tr, into next loop work 2 tr
3 ch and 2 tr, 1 tr into each of next 2 tr, 2 tr
into next sp, 1 tr into next tr; repeat from
★ omitting 1 tr at end of last repeat, 1 ss
into 3rd of 3 ch.

Second motif

Work as first motif for 2 rows.

3rd row 3 ch, 2 tr into next sp, 1 tr into
each of next 2 tr, 2 tr into next loop, 1 ch,
1 ss into corresponding loop on first motif,
1 ch, 2 tr into same loop on second motif,
1 tr into each of next 2 tr, 2 tr into next sp,
1 tr into next tr, 1 ss into corresponding tr
on first motif, 2 tr into next sp on second
motif, 1 tr into each of next 2 tr, 2 tr into
next loop, 1 ch, 1 ss into next loop on first
motif, 1 ch, 2 tr into same loop on second
motif and complete as for first motif.

Make 9 rows of 6 motifs, joining each as
second was joined to first. Where 4 corners
meet join third and fourth corners to
joining of previous motifs.

Damp and pin out to measurements.

Motif pattern bath mat *continued*

To make up

Cut towelling 21 in.× 30 in. Cut lining 21 in.× 30 in. Place crochet centrally on to towelling and slipstitch in position. Place towelling and lining right sides together and machine stitch ½ in. from the edges, leaving an opening sufficiently large to turn to right side. Slipstitch open edges together, or sew in position to bath mat.

Hot water bottle cover

Back and front (both alike)

Commence with 44 ch or a length of chain slightly wider than broadest part of bottle and having a multiple of 4.

1st row 1 dc into 2nd ch from hook, 1 dc into each ch, 1 ch, turn.

2nd row 1 dc into each dc, 1 ch, turn. Repeat second row 3 times more.

6th row 1 dc into each dc, 3 ch, turn.

7th row Miss first dc, 1 tr into each dc, 5 ch, turn.

8th row Miss first 2 tr, ★ 1 tr into each of next 3 tr, 2 ch, miss 1 tr; repeat from ★ 1 tr into 3rd of 3 ch, 5 ch, turn.

9th row Miss first tr and 2 ch, ★ 1 tr into next tr, 2 ch, miss 1 tr, 1 tr into next tr, 2 ch, miss 2 ch; repeat from ★ 1 tr into 3rd of 5 ch, 3 ch, turn.

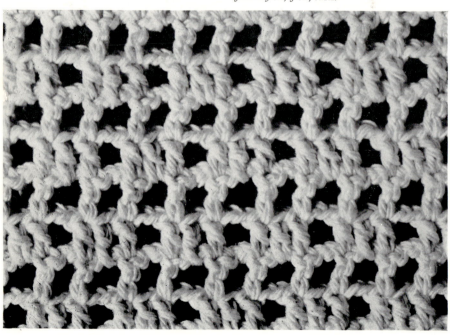

Coats 'Musica' Knitting Cotton, 2 oz Ready Wound Balls. 4 balls. Milward Disc (aluminium) crochet hook 3·50 (No. 9).
Hot Water Bottle, 11 in.×9 in.

Tension 5 rows of dc=1 in.
Measurements 12 in.×9¾ in.

10th row 1 tr into first sp, ★ 1 tr into next tr, 2 ch, miss 2 ch, 1 tr into next tr, 1 tr into next sp; repeat from ★ ending with 1 tr into 3rd of 5 ch, 5 ch, turn.

11th row Miss first 2 tr, ★ 1 tr into next tr, 2 ch, miss 2 ch, 1 tr into next tr, 2 ch, miss 1 tr; repeat from ★ ending with 1 tr into 3rd of 3 ch, 5 ch, turn.

12th row Miss first tr and 2 ch, ★ 1 tr into next tr, 1 tr into next sp, 1 tr into next tr, 2 ch, miss 2 ch; repeat from ★ 1 tr into 3rd of 5 ch, 5 ch, turn.

Repeat 9th to 12th row until work measures ¾ in. from base of bottle neck, ending with a 10th row, turning with 3 ch instead of 5 ch at end of last row.

Next row As 11th row omitting 2 ch at end of last repeat, 1 tr into 3rd of 3 ch, 3 ch, turn.

Next row Miss first tr, 1 tr into next tr, ★ 1 tr into next sp, 1 tr into next tr, 2 ch, miss 2 ch, 1 tr into next tr; repeat from ★ omitting 2 ch and 1 tr at end of last repeat, 1 tr into 3rd of 3 ch, 3 ch, turn.

Next row Miss first 3 tr, 1 tr into next tr, ★ 2 ch, miss 2 ch, 1 tr into next tr, 2 ch, miss 1 tr, 1 tr into next tr; repeat from ★ ending with 2 ch, miss 2 ch, 1 tr into next tr, 1 tr into 3rd of 3 ch, 3 ch, turn.

Next row Miss first tr, 1 tr into next tr, ★ 1 tr into next sp, 1 tr into next tr, 2 ch, miss 2 ch, 1 tr into next tr; repeat from ★ omitting 2 ch and 1 tr at end of last repeat, 1 tr into 3rd of 3 ch. Fasten off.

Cord

Commence with 141 ch.

1st row 1 dc into 2nd ch from hook, 1 dc into each dc.
Fasten off.

To make up

Place wrong sides together and join by a row of dc down each side working 3 dc into corner dc at each end of base of cover,

ss along base leaving opening for hook flap. Fasten off.

Frill

1st row Attach thread to first sp after seam, 2 dc into same place as join, ★ 1 dc into each of next 3 tr, 2 dc into next sp; repeat from ★ to within 3 tr of next seam, 1 dc into each of next 3 tr, 1 dc into first dc of side seam; repeat from ★ to within 3 tr of first seam, 1 dc into each of next 3 tr, 1 dc into first dc of next side seam, 1 dc into each of next 3 tr.

2nd to 5th row 1 dc into each dc, ending last row with a ss into first dc.
Fasten off.

128